CUT AND CREATE!

AT THE ZOO

EASY STEP-BY-STEP PROJECTS THAT TEACH SCISSOR SKILLS

Teaching & Learning Company

1204 Buchanan St., P.O. Box 10
Carthage, IL 62321

This book belongs to

_____

This book was developed for the Teaching & Learning Company by The Good Neighbor Press, Inc., Grand Junction, CO.

Cover by Nancee Jean McClure

Teaching & Learning Company
1204 Buchanan St., P.O. Box 10
Carthage, IL 62321

TABLE OF CONTENTS

Dear Teacher or Parent,

*C*ut and Create! At the Zoo was developed to provide you, the parent or classroom teacher, with activities that will serve your young children in two ways:

1) provide easy step-by-step projects that develop scissor skills and reinforce visual-motor coordination, and

2) supplement your art program with activities that are fun and colorful, have great display possibilities and use materials that are readily available.

Amazingly simple, fun activities like the ones included in this book will help your early childhood students build a solid foundation for well-developed information processing skills. The process of completing a *Cut and Create* activity will require your students to observe and discriminate the separate parts of the animal they're creating and their relationship to one another. Each activity becomes an enjoyable challenge to generate cognitive knowledge!

Structured, sequential activities are *not* intended to take the place of a developmentally appropriate process-oriented art program. However, these scissor skill activities are very useful in achieving the following:

- Developing manual dexterity and patterns of movement

- Encouraging social communicability

- Helping the child to master his environment by controlling tools and materials

- Encouraging observation

- Developing discrimination of color, shape and texture

- Stimulating students' imaginations

- Developing skills necessary for mathematical thinking such as grouping, ordering and spatial orientation

We hope you and your students enjoy the scissor skill activities in *Cut and Create!* They're simple, easy to implement and fun to create!

PANDA

1 Cut a #1 circle from white paper.

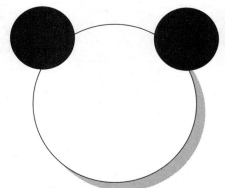

2 Cut two #2 circles from black construction paper and glue them as shown onto the white circle.

3 Cut two #3 circles from black paper, two #4 circles from white paper, and two #5 circles from black paper. Glue them into a concentric pattern as shown.

4 Cut one #6 circle from white paper and glue as shown.

5 Cut one #7 triangle from black paper and glue it on the top, center of the panda's muzzle.

6 Use a black crayon or marker to add an upper lip and a smile to the panda.

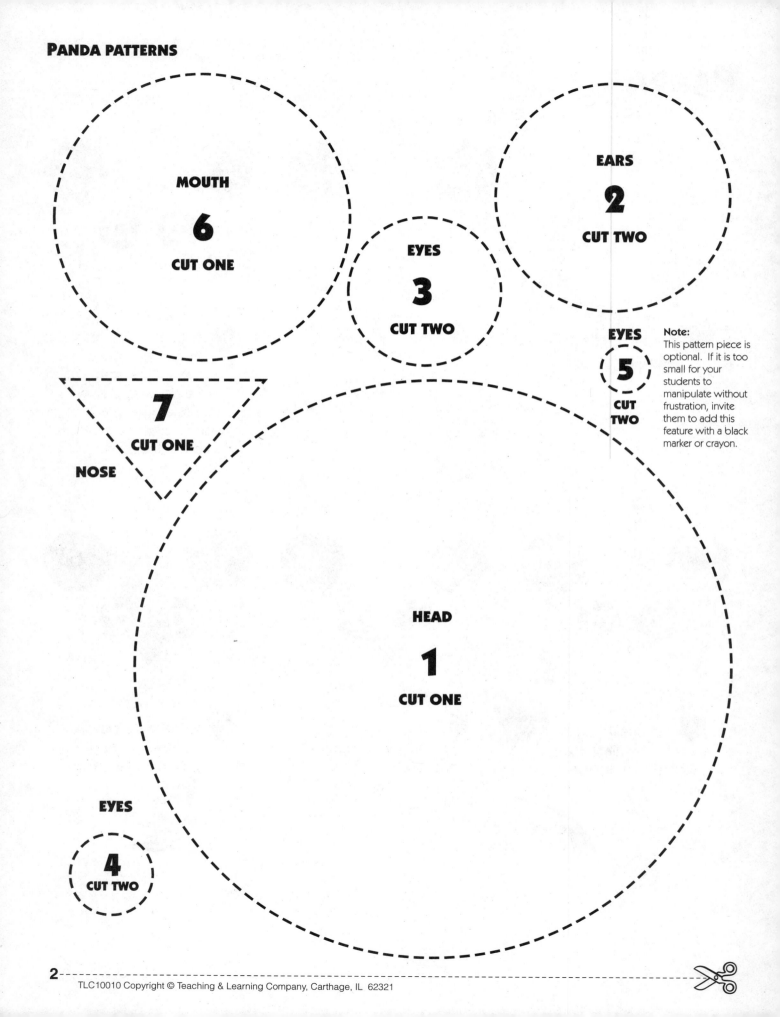

TIGER

Materials: *white, black, orange and brown paper; scissors; glue; crayons; markers*
Optional Materials: *pipe cleaners or broom straw*

1 Cut one #1 circle from orange paper and two #2 circles from white paper. Glue the white circles as shown.

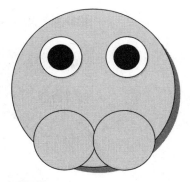

2 Cut two #3 circles from black paper and two #4 circles from orange paper. Glue as shown.

3 Cut two #5 circles from orange paper and two #6 circles from black paper. Glue the black circles onto the orange circles.

4 Glue the ears to the underside of the tiger's face. Cut one #7 triangle from brown paper and glue it onto the face.

5 Cut out and glue the #8 triangle from black paper. Glue as shown. Create tiger stripes by either cutting and gluing the #9 patterns or using a black crayon or marker.

6 Use a black crayon or marker to add a smile and "freckles." You can also make whiskers from broom straw or pipe cleaners.

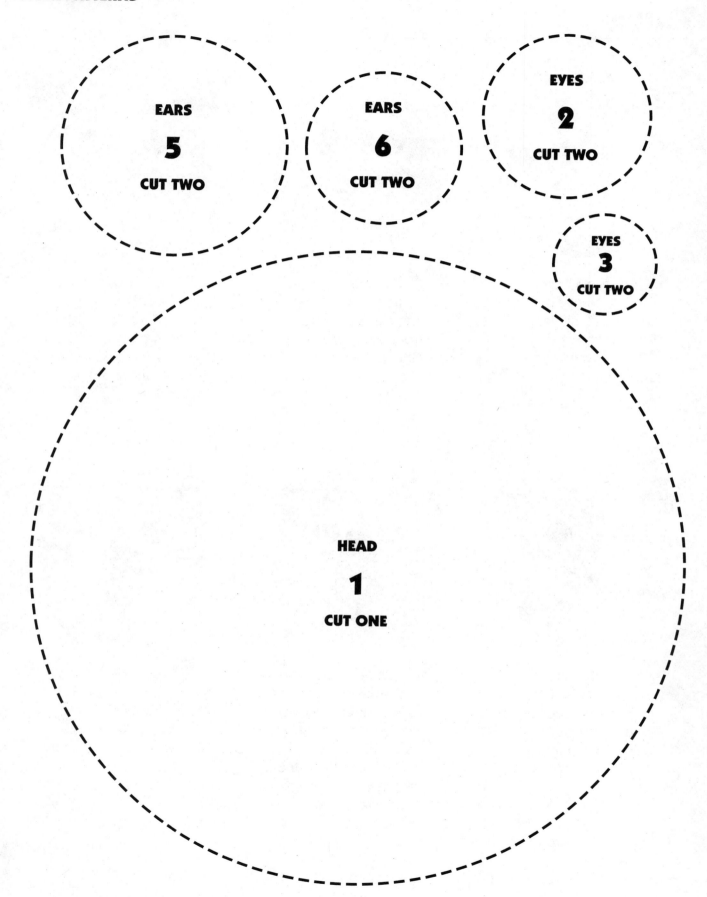

EARS

5

CUT TWO

EARS

6

CUT TWO

EYES

2

CUT TWO

EYES

3

CUT TWO

HEAD

1

CUT ONE

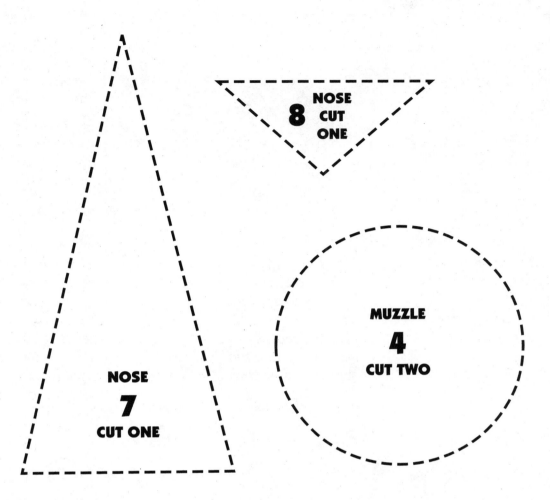

NOSE

8 CUT ONE

NOSE

7

CUT ONE

MUZZLE

4

CUT TWO

TIGER STRIPES

9

CUT TWO OF EACH

Note:
These pattern pieces are optional. If they are too small for your students to cut, add the tiger stripes with a black crayon or marker.

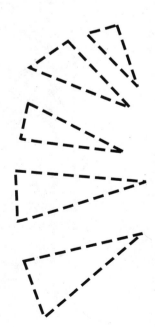

Note:
This is how the tiger's mouth is rendered. Use it to trace or copy.

Materials: *gray, white, black and pink paper; scissors; glue*

HIPPOPOTAMUS

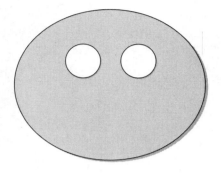

1 Cut a #1 oval from gray paper. Cut two #2 circles from white paper and glue them onto the oval as shown.

2 Cut two #3 eyes from black paper and glue them onto the center of the #2 eyes. Cut two #4 ears from gray paper and glue them as shown.

3 Cut the #6 pattern piece from gray paper and glue it to the head, slightly overlapping the eyes. Add the #5 ears from pink paper and glue them on top of the #4 ears.

4 Cut two #7 nostrils from pink paper and glue them onto the muzzle.

5 Cut the #8 smile from black paper and glue onto the muzzle.

6 Cut out four #9 teeth from white paper and glue them onto the mouth.

TLC10010 Copyright © Teaching & Learning Company, Carthage, IL 62321

HIPPOPOTAMUS PATTERNS

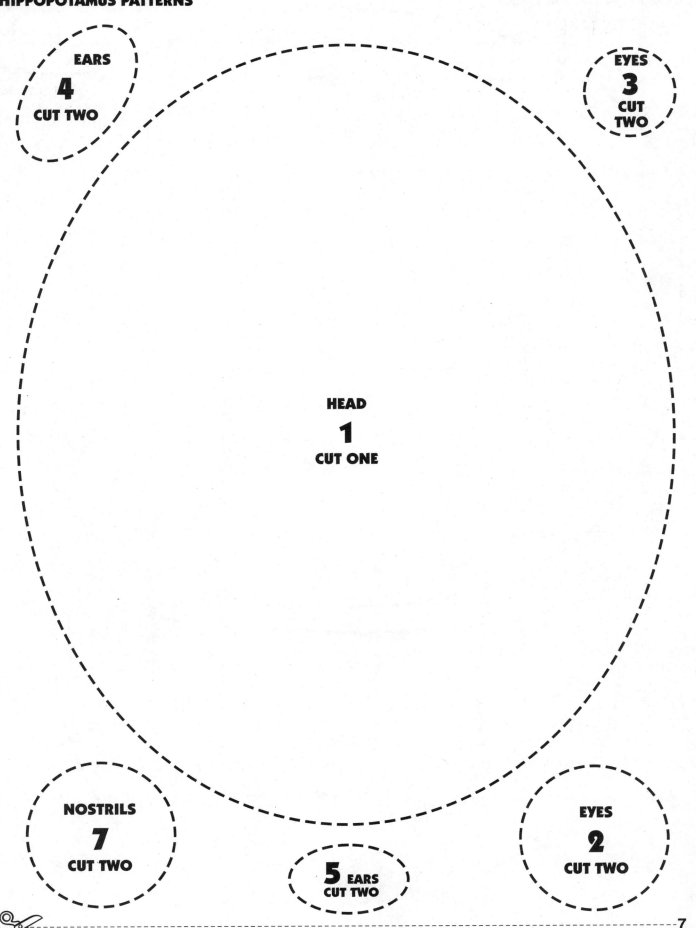

EARS
4
CUT TWO

EYES
3
CUT
TWO

HEAD
1
CUT ONE

NOSTRILS
7
CUT TWO

5 EARS
CUT TWO

EYES
2
CUT TWO

Hippopotamus Patterns

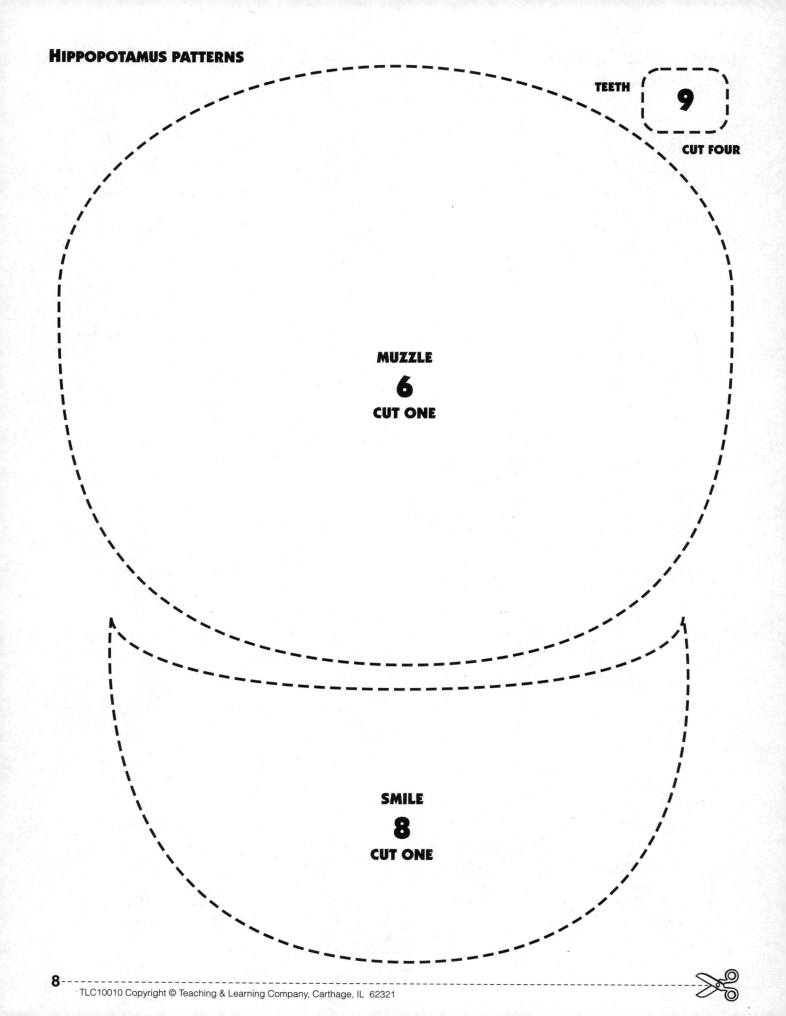

TEETH

9

CUT FOUR

MUZZLE

6

CUT ONE

SMILE

8

CUT ONE

Hippopotamus Patterns

LION

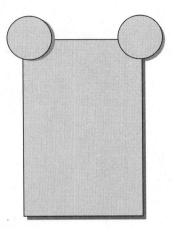

1 Cut a #1 rectangle from tan paper. Cut two #2 ears from tan paper and glue them to the head.

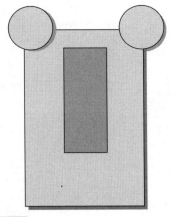

2 Cut the #3 rectangle from brown paper and glue it to the head as shown.

3 Cut two #4 eyes from white paper and glue them, overlapping the nose.

4 Cut two #5 ears from brown paper and glue them, centered, onto the ears. Cut two #6 eyes from black paper and glue them, centered, onto the #4 eyes.

5 Cut two #7 muzzles from brown paper and glue them, as shown, onto the head. Cut one #8 nose from black paper and glue it to the bottom edge of the #3 nose.

6 Use a black crayon or marker to draw the lion's smile and "freckles." Glue tan strips (#9 pattern) of paper around the lion's face, creating a mane.

MANE
9

HEAD
1
CUT ONE

Note:
The illustration shows 29 mane strips. Cutting this many pieces will be too daunting for most young children. Pre-cut these strips using a paper cutter before you begin this activity. You could also pre-cut yarn strips to create a mane.

LION PATTERNS

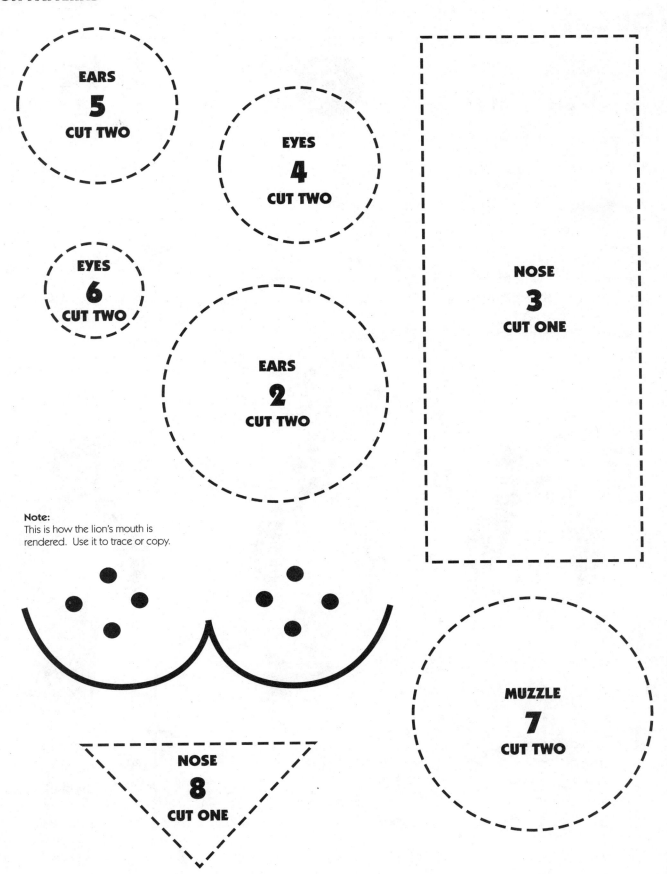

EARS
5
CUT TWO

EYES
4
CUT TWO

EYES
6
CUT TWO

NOSE
3
CUT ONE

EARS
2
CUT TWO

Note:
This is how the lion's mouth is
rendered. Use it to trace or copy.

MUZZLE
7
CUT TWO

NOSE
8
CUT ONE

Materials: *white, black, yellow and green paper; scissors; glue; crayons or markers*

TOUCAN

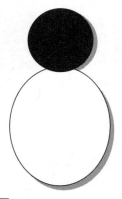

1 Begin by cutting one #1 body from white paper and one #2 head from black paper. Glue the head to the body.

2 Cut one #3 eye from bright green paper and one #4 eye from black paper. Glue the black circle onto the green circle, then glue both slightly to the right of the center of the head.

3 Cut one #5 bill from yellow paper and glue it to the head.

4 Cut two #6 wings from black paper and glue them to the toucan as shown.

5 Cut one #7 tail from black paper and glue it to the underside of the body.

6 Cut two #8 feet from the yellow paper and glue them as shown. Draw three vertical lines on each foot with a black crayon or marker.

Toucan Patterns

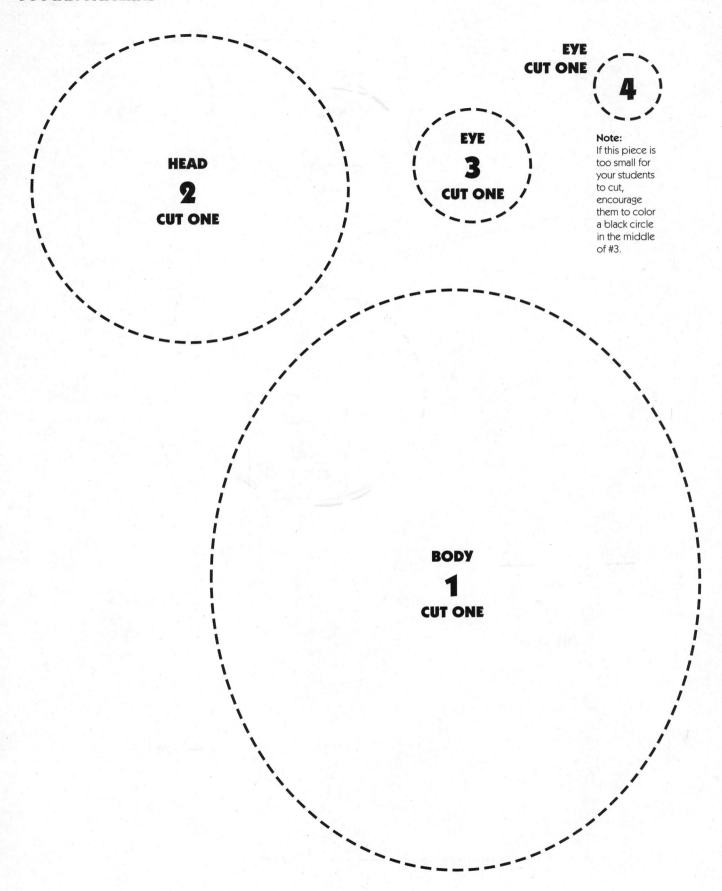

HEAD
2
CUT ONE

EYE
3
CUT ONE

EYE
CUT ONE
4

Note:
If this piece is too small for your students to cut, encourage them to color a black circle in the middle of #3.

BODY
1
CUT ONE

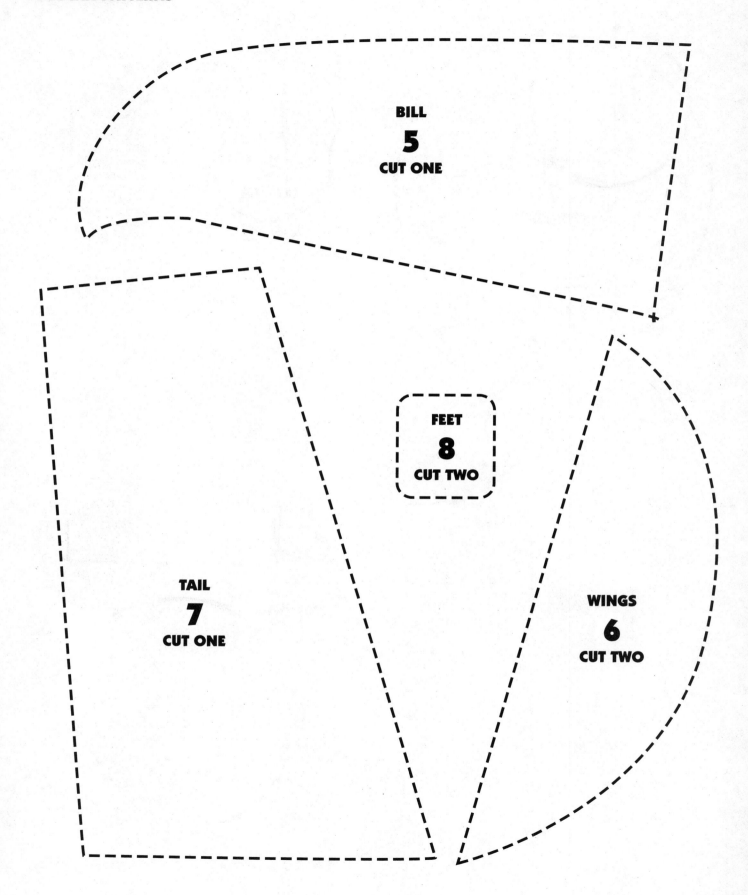

BILL
5
CUT ONE

FEET
8
CUT TWO

TAIL
7
CUT ONE

WINGS
6
CUT TWO

Materials: *tan and black paper; scissors; glue; crayons or markers*

KOALA

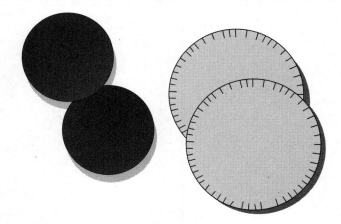

1 Begin by cutting two #1 ears from black paper. Cut two #2 circles from tan paper. Encourage your students to make small cuts with their scissors along the outside edge of the tan pattern pieces, as illustrated. Glue the black pieces to the center of the tan pieces.

2 Cut one #3 head from tan paper. Glue the ears to the underside of the head as shown.

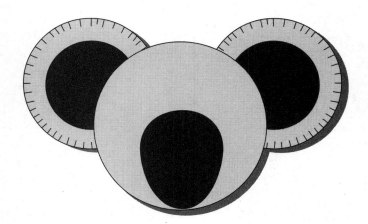

3 Cut one #4 nose from black paper. Glue it to the head as illustrated.

4 Cut two #5 eyes from black paper. Because this is a small piece, some of your students may prefer to add the eyes with a black marker or crayon. Using the crayon or marker, add three eyelashes to each eye and a smile.

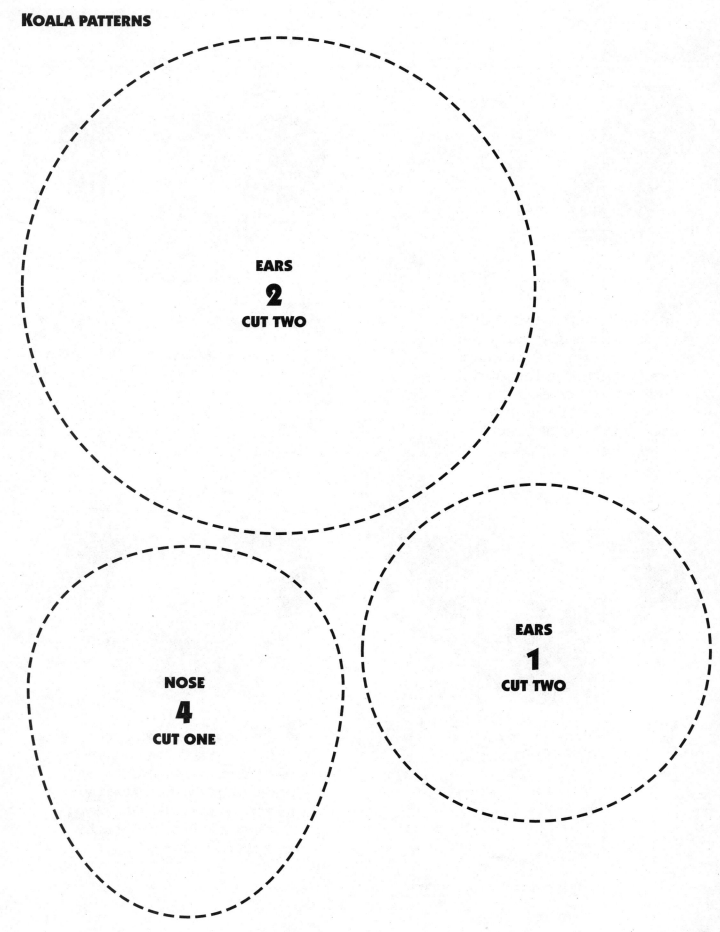

EARS
2
CUT TWO

NOSE
4
CUT ONE

EARS
1
CUT TWO

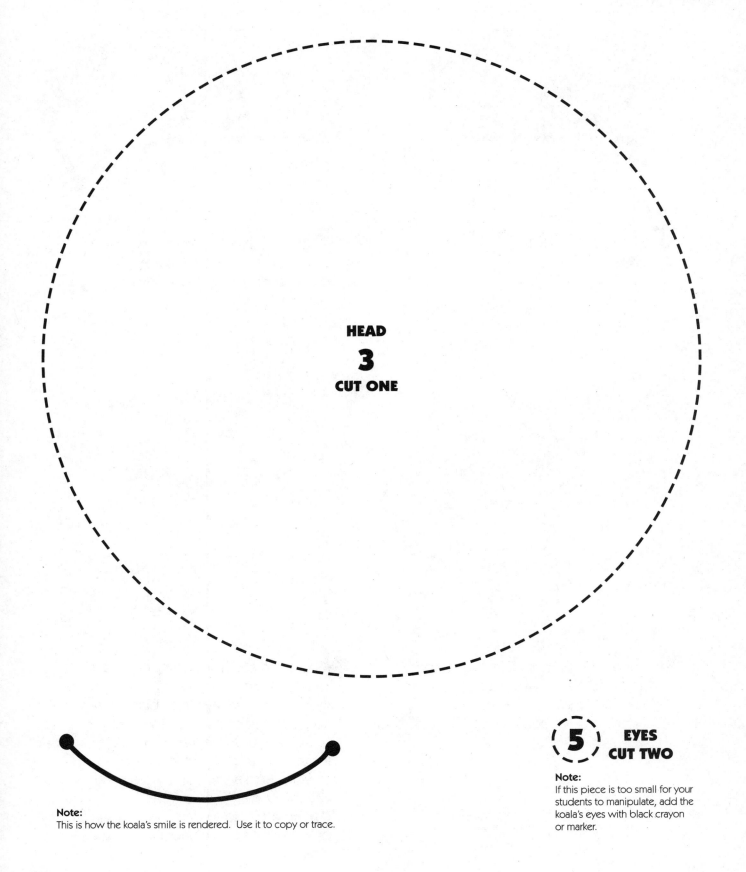

HEAD
3
CUT ONE

5 EYES
CUT TWO

Note:
If this piece is too small for your students to manipulate, add the koala's eyes with black crayon or marker.

Note:
This is how the koala's smile is rendered. Use it to copy or trace.

WHALE

Materials: *pink and light blue paper, scissors, glue, black marker or crayon*
Optional Materials: *pipe cleaners*

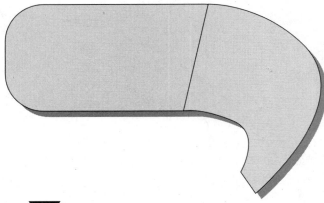

1 Cut one #1 body from light blue paper.

2 Cut one #2 body from light blue paper. Glue it to the rectangular piece, overlapping the rectangular piece as shown.

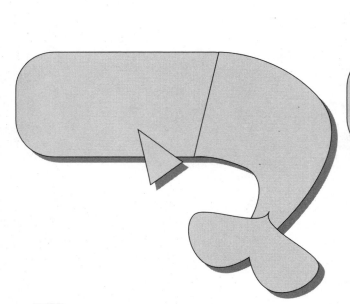

3 Cut one #3 tail from light blue paper and glue it as shown. Cut one #4 flipper from light blue paper and glue it to the rectangular body piece.

4 Cut one #5 cheek from pink paper and glue it on top of the point of the flipper. Cut a #6 eye from black paper and glue it as shown. If this piece is too small for your students to manipulate, invite them to draw the eye with black crayon. Add a smile and a blowhole with black marker or crayon.
Optional: Add a waterspout by gluing pipe cleaners to the underside of the whale.

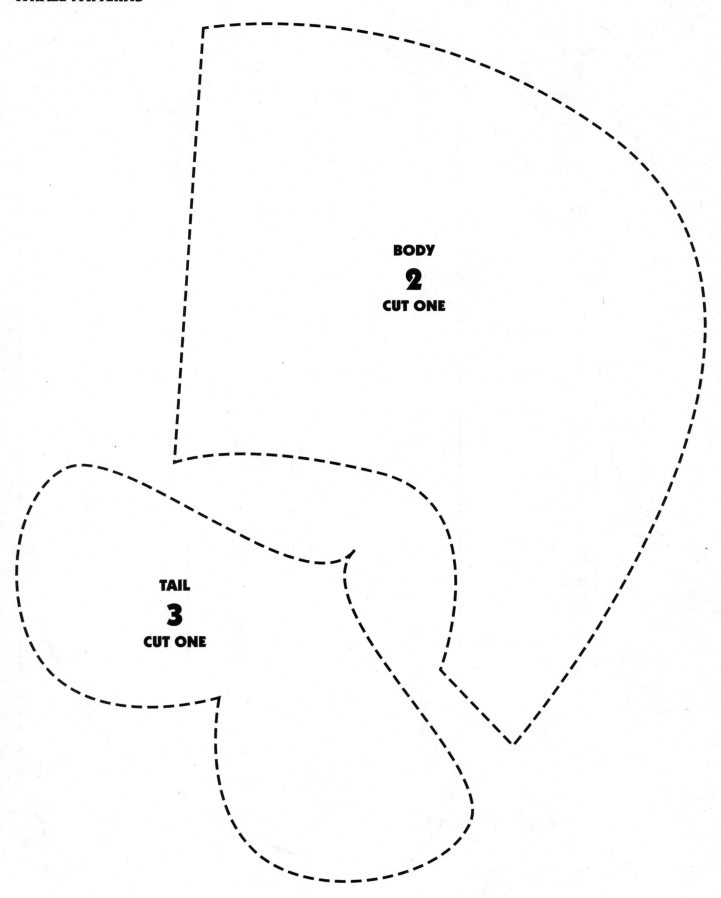

BODY

2

CUT ONE

TAIL

3

CUT ONE

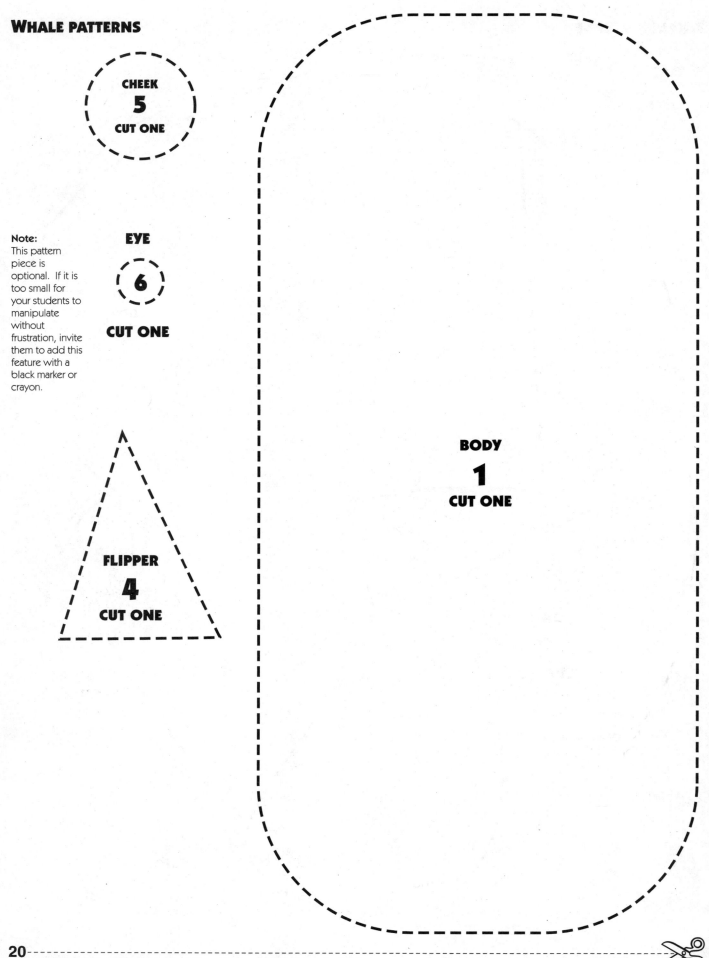

CHEEK
5
CUT ONE

EYE
6
CUT ONE

Note:
This pattern piece is optional. If it is too small for your students to manipulate without frustration, invite them to add this feature with a black marker or crayon.

FLIPPER
4
CUT ONE

BODY
1
CUT ONE

BABOON

Materials: brown, red, blue, black and white paper; black marker or crayon; scissors; glue

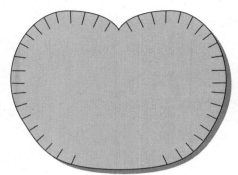

1 Cut one #1 mane from brown paper. Invite your students to use their scissors and make small cuts all the way around the mane as illustrated.

2 Cut one #2 head from blue paper and glue it to the mane as shown.

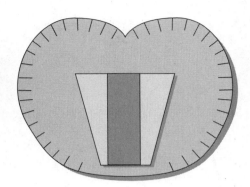

3 Cut one #3 nose from red paper and glue it to the head as shown.

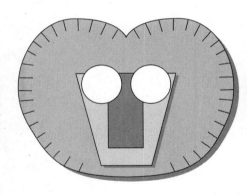

4 Cut two #4 eyes from white paper. Glue them as illustrated onto the baboon's face.

5 Cut two #5 eyes from black paper. Glue them to the center of the #4 eyes. Cut one #6 muzzle from red paper and glue it to the bottom of the face. With a black crayon or marker, add a vertical line on either side of the #3 nose.

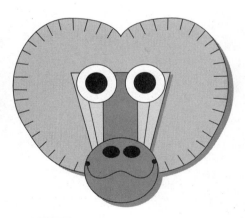

6 Cut two #7 nostrils from black paper and glue them to the red muzzle as shown. If this piece is too small for your students to manipulate, encourage them to draw the nostrils with a black crayon or marker. Add a smile with a black crayon or marker.

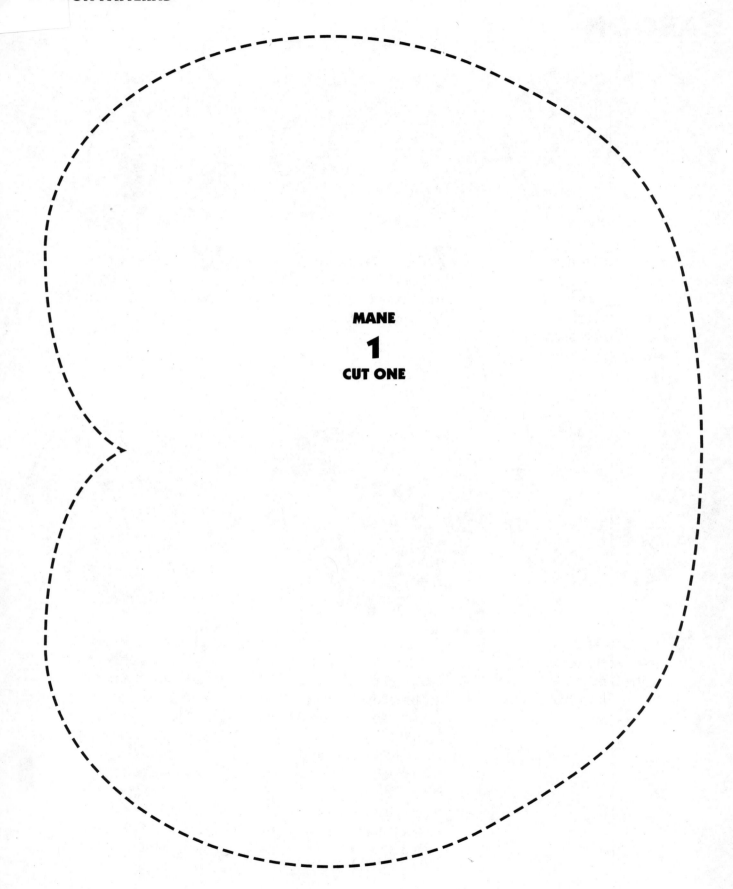

MANE

1

CUT ONE

ЭON PATTERNS

BABOON PATTERNS

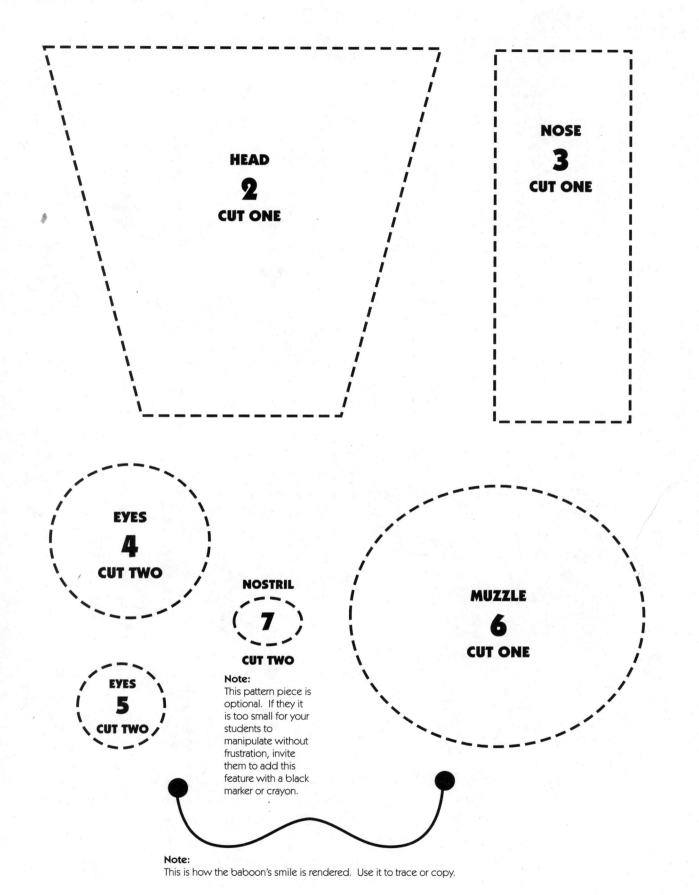

HEAD
2
CUT ONE

NOSE
3
CUT ONE

EYES
4
CUT TWO

EYES
5
CUT TWO

NOSTRIL
7
CUT TWO

Note:
This pattern piece is optional. If they it is too small for your students to manipulate without frustration, invite them to add this feature with a black marker or crayon.

MUZZLE
6
CUT ONE

Note:
This is how the baboon's smile is rendered. Use it to trace or copy.

Materials: gray and pink paper, scissors, glue, black crayon or marker

ELEPHANT

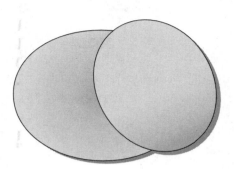

1 Begin by cutting one #1 body and one #2 ear from gray paper. Glue the ear onto the body as shown.

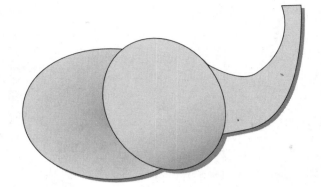

2 Cut one #3 trunk from gray paper and glue it to the underside of the ear as shown.

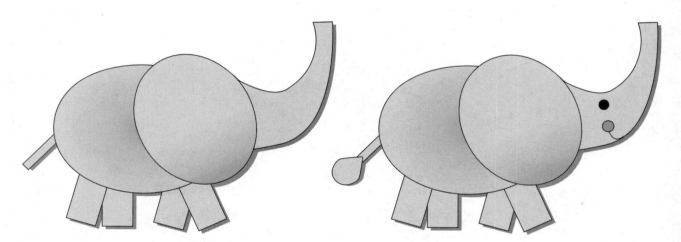

3 Cut four #4 legs from gray paper and glue them to the bottom, underside of the elephant's body. Cut one #5 tail and glue it to the underside of the elephant as shown.

4 Cut one #6 tail from gray paper and glue it to the end of the #5 tail. Cut one #7 cheek from pink paper and glue as shown. Cut one #8 eye from black paper and glue it above the cheek. These last two features may also be added with marker or crayon. Add a smile with a black crayon or marker.

Elephant patterns

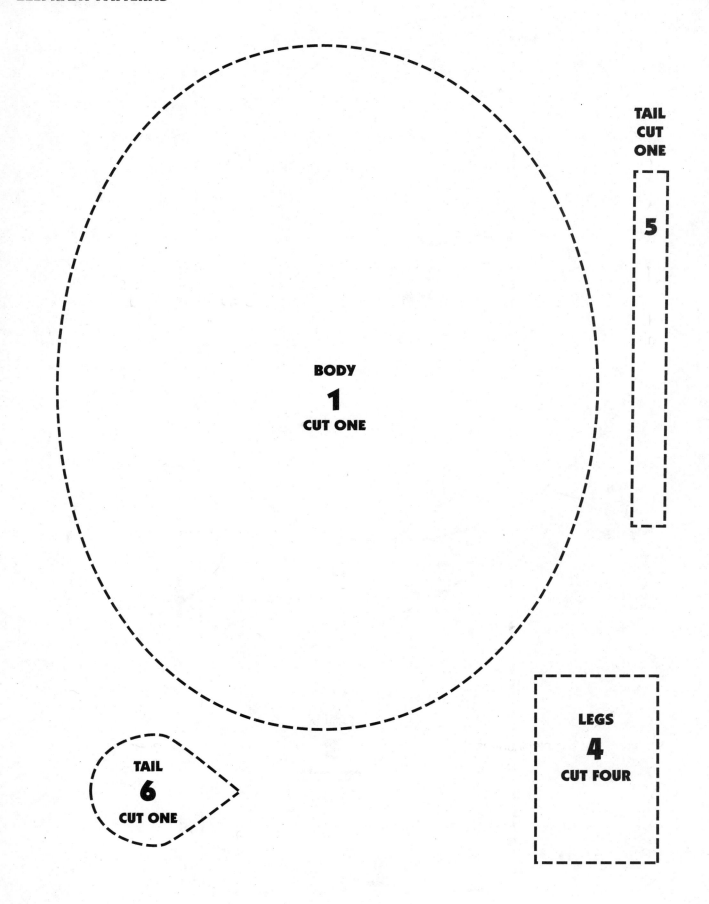

TAIL
CUT
ONE

5

BODY

1

CUT ONE

LEGS

4

CUT FOUR

TAIL

6

CUT ONE

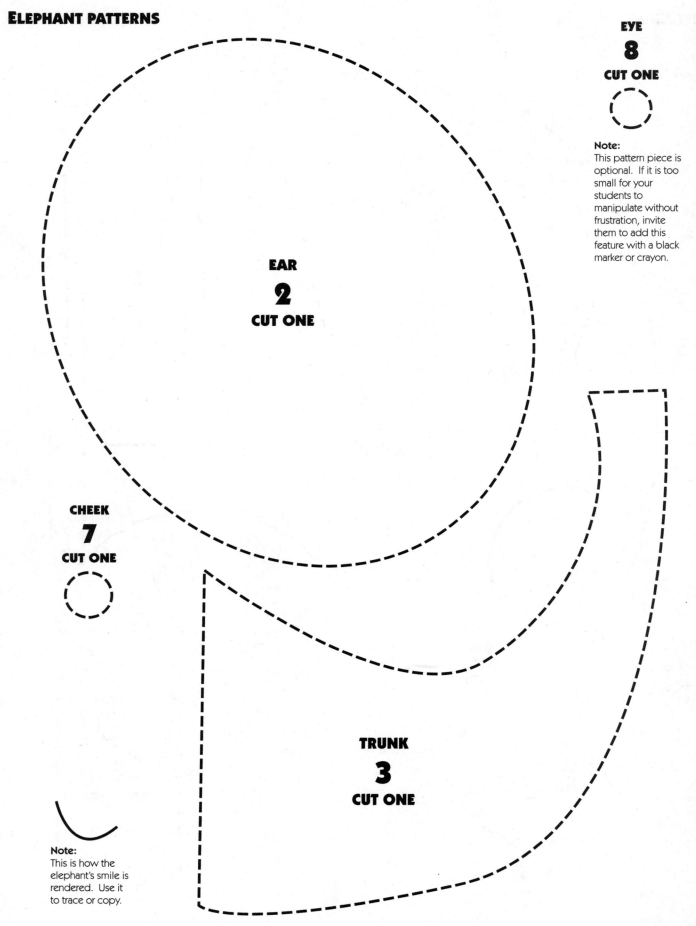

EYE

8

CUT ONE

Note:
This pattern piece is optional. If it is too small for your students to manipulate without frustration, invite them to add this feature with a black marker or crayon.

EAR

2

CUT ONE

CHEEK

7

CUT ONE

TRUNK

3

CUT ONE

Note:
This is how the elephant's smile is rendered. Use it to trace or copy.

Materials: *yellow, brown, white and tan paper; scissors; glue; black crayon or marker*

PELICAN

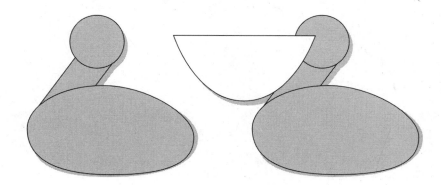

1 Cut one #1 body from tan paper. Cut one #2 neck from tan paper and glue it to the underside of the body as shown.

2 Cut one #3 head from tan paper and glue it to the top of the neck.

3 Cut one #4 bill from yellow paper and glue it to the left edge of the neck and head.

4 Cut one #5 eye from white paper and glue it to the right tip of the bill, as shown. Cut one #6 wing from brown paper and glue it to the body.

5 Cut two #7 feet from yellow paper and glue them to the underside of the body as shown. Cut one #8 eye from black paper and glue it to the center of the white portion of the eye. If this piece is too small for your students to manipulate, invite them to draw a circle on the white of the eye using black crayon or marker.

6 Add some "feathers" on the wing with a black crayon or marker. Add a smile to the pelican's bill with a black crayon or marker.

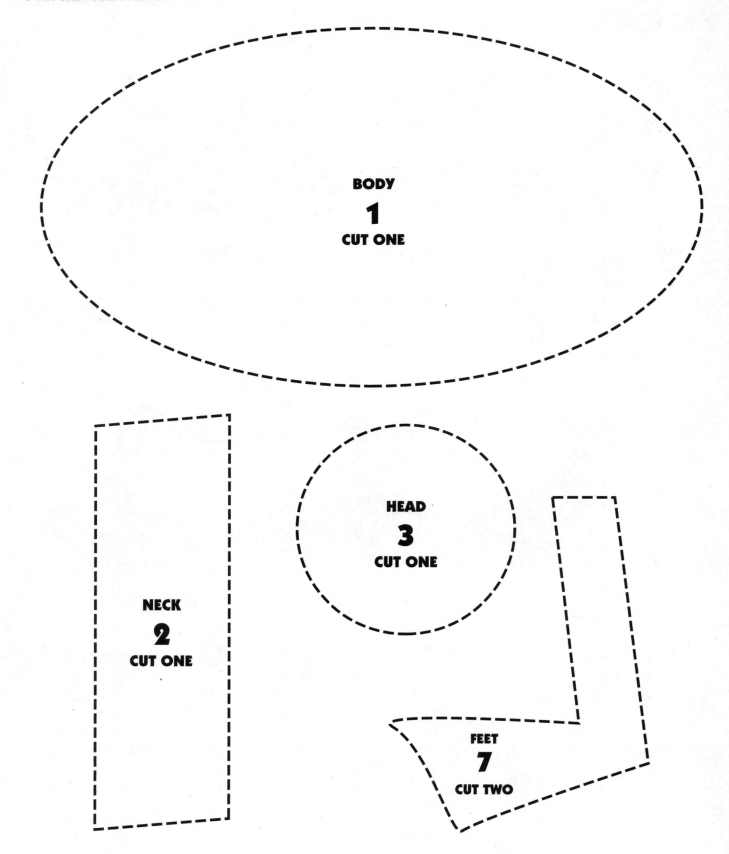

BODY
1
CUT ONE

HEAD
3
CUT ONE

NECK
2
CUT ONE

FEET
7
CUT TWO

PELICAN PATTERNS

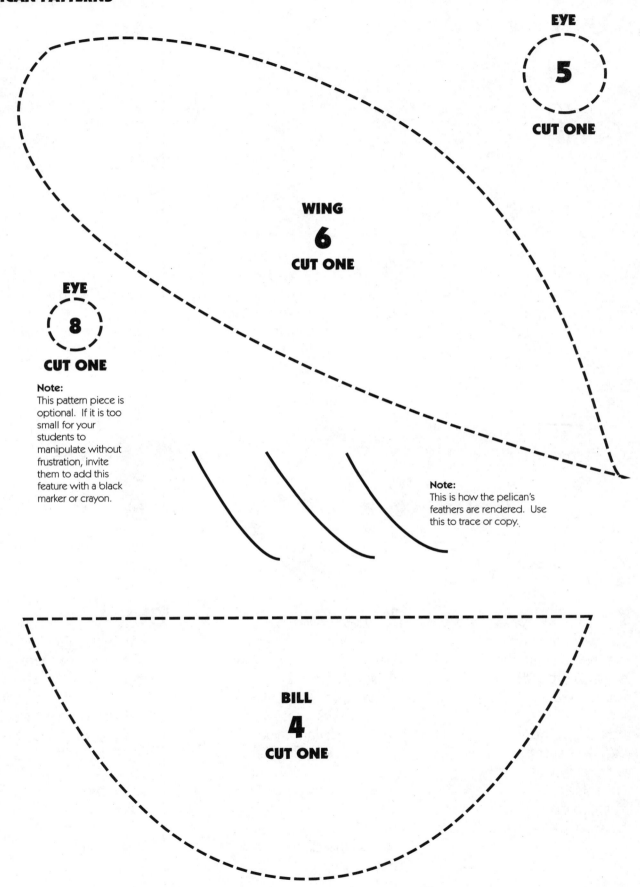

EYE

5

CUT ONE

WING

6

CUT ONE

EYE

8

CUT ONE

Note:
This pattern piece is optional. If it is too small for your students to manipulate without frustration, invite them to add this feature with a black marker or crayon.

Note:
This is how the pelican's feathers are rendered. Use this to trace or copy.

BILL

4

CUT ONE

Materials: *light green, green, white and black paper; scissors; glue; black crayon or marker*

IGUANA

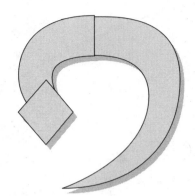

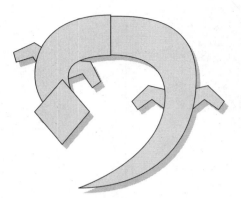

1 Begin by cutting one #1 body from light green paper. Then cut one #2 tail from light green paper. Glue the body to the tail.

2 Cut one #3 head from light green paper. Glue it onto the body as shown.

3 Cut two #4 leg pieces from light green paper and glue them to the underside of the body as shown.

4 Cut two #5 eyes from white paper and glue them to the head. Cut four #6 feet from dark green paper and glue each one to the ends of the four legs. This piece is optional if your students are too young to manipulate this small piece.

5 Cut three #7 diamonds from dark green paper. Glue them to the body as shown. Cut two #8 eyes from black paper and glue them to the white part of the iguana's eyes. If your students are too young to manipulate this piece, invite them to add this detail with black marker or crayon.

6 Cut two #9 circles from dark green paper and glue them to the iguana's tail as shown. Again, this detail can be omitted or added with crayon or marker. Add a smile and nostrils with black crayon or marker.

IGUANA PATTERNS

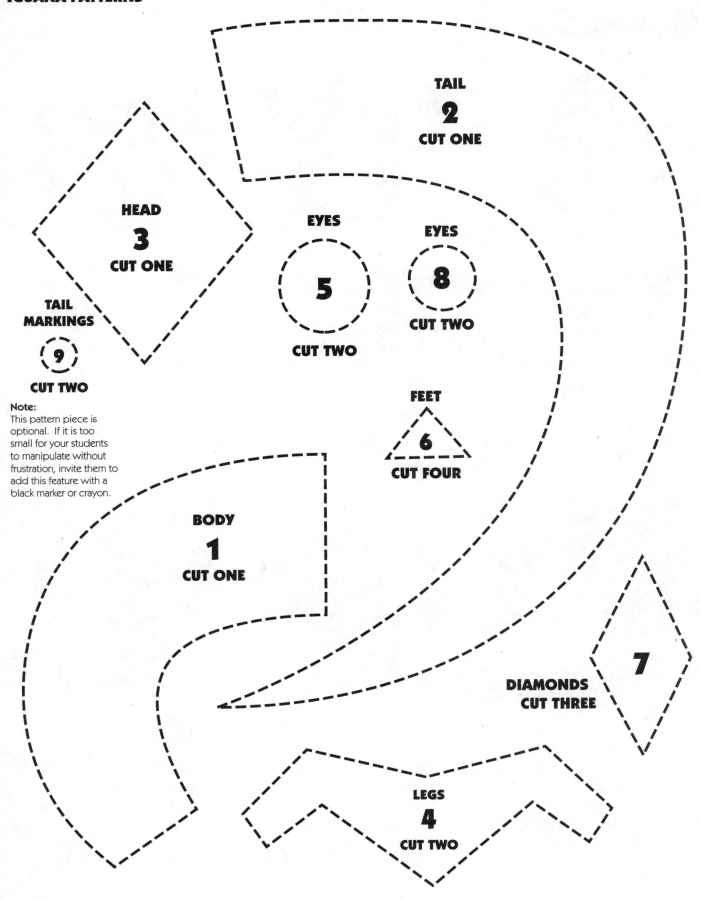

TAIL
2
CUT ONE

HEAD
3
CUT ONE

EYES
5
CUT TWO

EYES
8
CUT TWO

TAIL MARKINGS
9
CUT TWO

Note:
This pattern piece is optional. If it is too small for your students to manipulate without frustration, invite them to add this feature with a black marker or crayon.

FEET
6
CUT FOUR

BODY
1
CUT ONE

DIAMONDS
CUT THREE
7

LEGS
4
CUT TWO

Materials: *black, brown, tan and white paper; scissors; glue; black crayon or marker*

GORILLA

1 Cut one #1 head from brown paper. Cut one #2 nose from tan paper and glue it to the head as shown.

2 Cut two #3 ears from brown paper. Cut two #4 ears from black paper and glue them, centered, to the #3 ears.

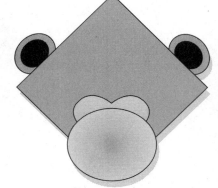

3 Glue the ears to the underside of the head. Cut one #5 mouth from tan paper and glue it to the head as shown.

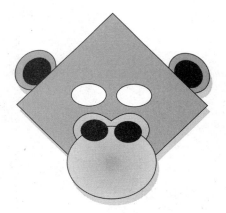

4 Cut two #6 nostrils from black paper and glue them to the nose as shown. Cut two #7 eyes from white paper and glue them to the head.

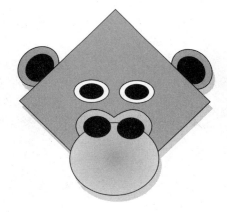

5 Cut two #8 eyes from black paper and glue them on top of the #7 eyes.

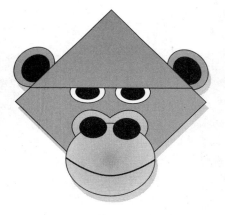

6 Cut one #9 forehead from brown paper and glue it to the head, overlapping the top of the eyes. Draw a smile on the mouth with black crayon or marker.

GORILLA PATTERNS

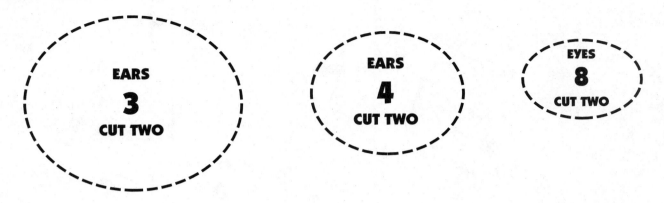

EARS
3
CUT TWO

EARS
4
CUT TWO

EYES
8
CUT TWO

HEAD
1
CUT ONE

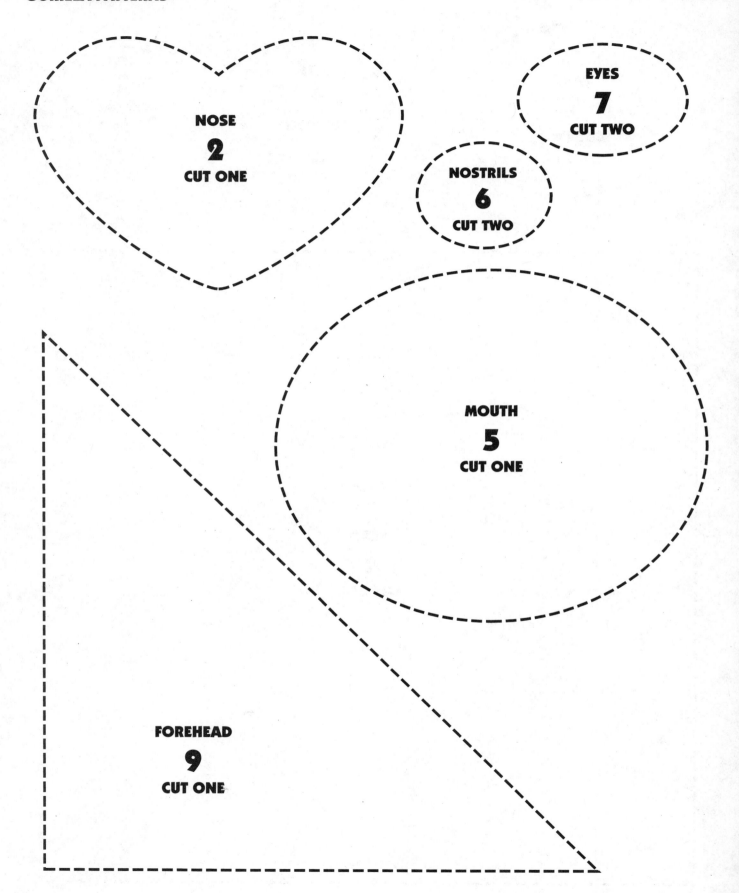

NOSE
2
CUT ONE

EYES
7
CUT TWO

NOSTRILS
6
CUT TWO

MOUTH
5
CUT ONE

FOREHEAD
9
CUT ONE

SHARK

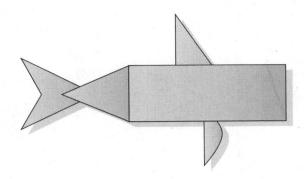

1 Cut one #1 body from gray paper. Cut one #2 body from gray paper and glue it to the underside of the #1 body.

2 Cut one #3 tail from gray paper and glue it to the underside of the #2 body. Cut one #4 fin from gray paper and glue it to the underside of the body as shown. Cut one #5 fin from gray paper and glue it to the underside of the body as shown.

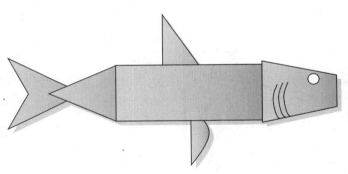

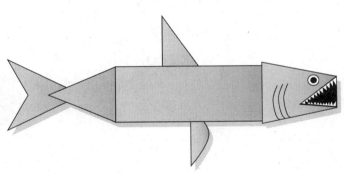

3 Cut one #6 head and glue it to the #1 body as shown. Cut one #7 eye from white paper and glue it on the head. Draw three gills on the head as shown.

4 With a black marker or crayon add a black circle to the white of the shark's eye. Draw the outline of a triangle on the shark's head as shown. Then draw pointed teeth on the top and bottom jaw. Color in the rest of the mouth with black marker or crayon.

SHARK PATTERNS

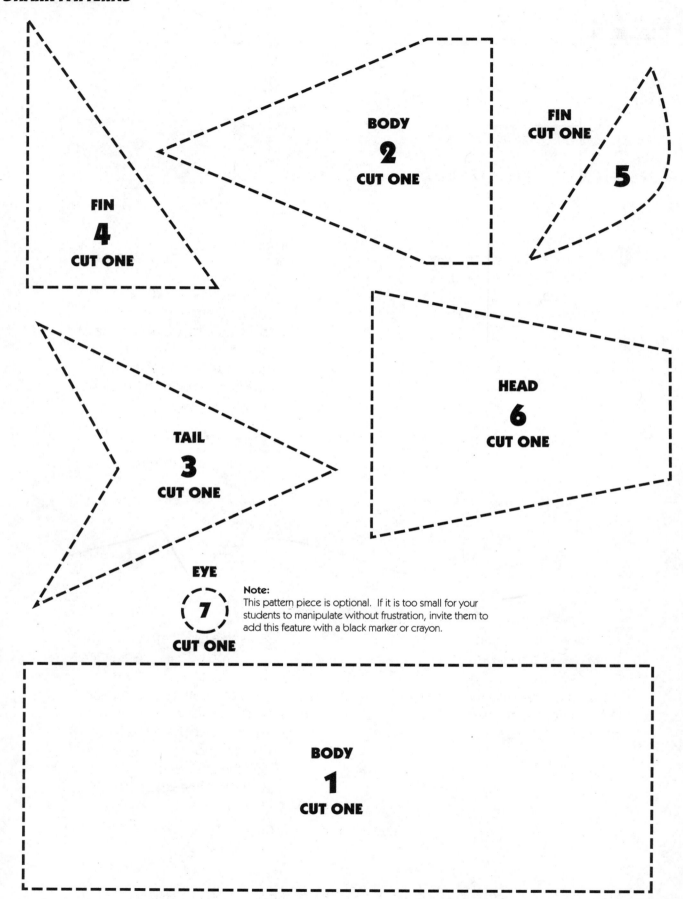

BODY
2
CUT ONE

FIN
CUT ONE
5

FIN
4
CUT ONE

HEAD
6
CUT ONE

TAIL
3
CUT ONE

EYE
7
CUT ONE

Note:
This pattern piece is optional. If it is too small for your students to manipulate without frustration, invite them to add this feature with a black marker or crayon.

BODY
1
CUT ONE

Materials: *green, red, yellow and black paper; scissors; glue*

TURTLE

1 Cut one #1 shell from black paper. Cut one #2 shell from red paper. Glue it to the center of the black shell.

2 Cut four #3 feet from green paper. Glue them to the underside of the black oval as shown.

3 Cut one #4 head from green paper and glue it to the underside of the black oval.

4 Cut two #5 eyes from white paper and glue them to either side of the head as shown. Cut four #6 triangles from green paper and glue them onto the red shell as shown.

5 Cut two #7 eyes from black paper and glue them to the white part of the eyes. Cut four #8 triangles from yellow paper and glue them to the red shell as shown.

6 Cut one #9 oval from black paper and glue it to the shell, overlapping all of the triangles. With a black crayon or marker, add a smile to the turtle's face.

 TLC10010 Copyright © Teaching & Learning Company, Carthage, IL 62321

TURTLE PATTERNS

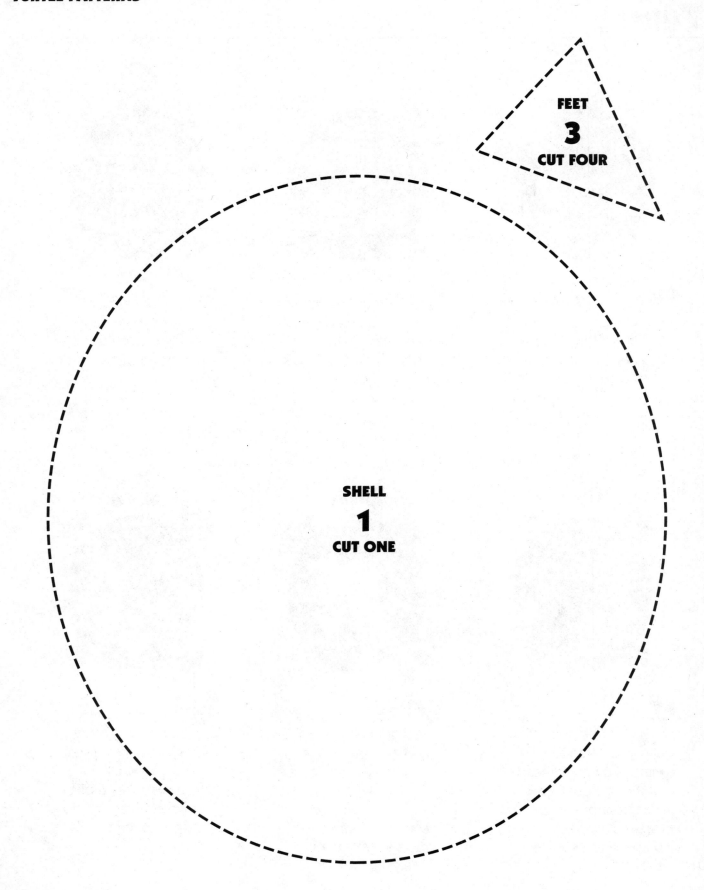

FEET
3
CUT FOUR

SHELL
1
CUT ONE

TURTLE PATTERNS

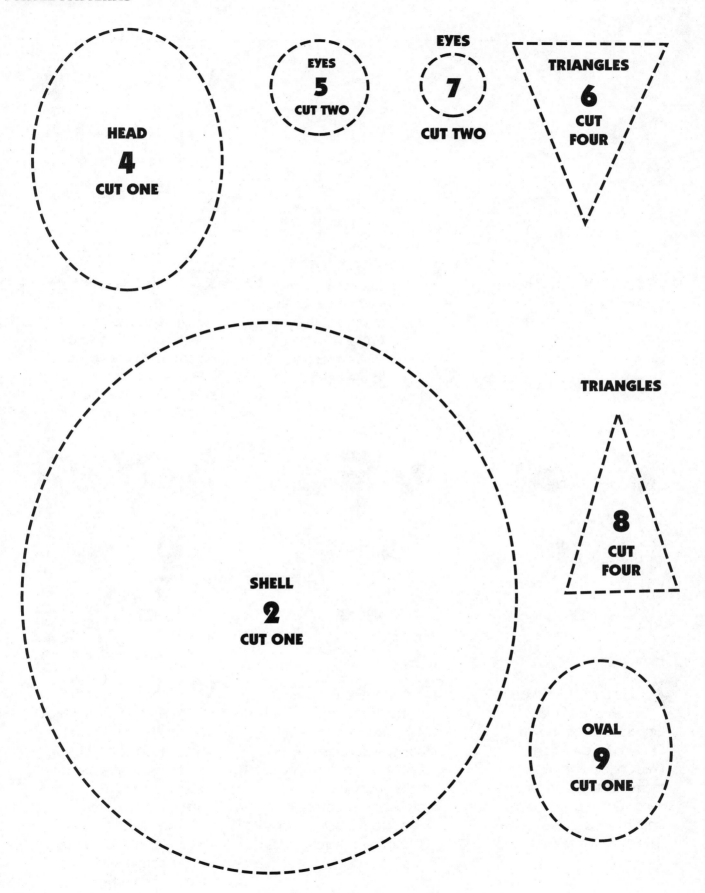

HEAD
4
CUT ONE

EYES
5
CUT TWO

EYES
7
CUT TWO

TRIANGLES
6
CUT FOUR

SHELL
2
CUT ONE

TRIANGLES
8
CUT FOUR

OVAL
9
CUT ONE

Materials: black and white paper, scissors, glue

ZEBRA

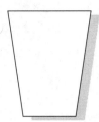

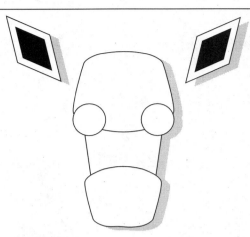

▼**1** Cut one #1 head from white paper.

▼**2** Cut one #2 forehead from white paper and glue it to the zebra's head. Cut one #3 nose from white paper and glue it to the head as shown.

▼**3** Cut two #4 eyes from white paper and glue them to the head as shown. Cut two #5 ears from white paper. Cut two #6 ears from black paper and glue them, centered, to the #5 ears.

▼**4** Glue the ears to the underside of the zebra's head as shown. Cut two #7 eyes from black paper and glue them, centered, to the #4 eyes. Cut two #8 nostrils from black paper and glue them to the nose as shown.

▼**5** Cut one #10 mane from black paper. Make several cuts along the top with scissors, as shown. Glue the mane to the underside of the forehead. Cut one #11 blaze from black paper. Glue it to the forehead as shown.

▼**6** Cut two sets of the #12 stripes from black paper. Glue them to the head as shown. If these pieces are too small for your students to manipulate, invite them to color black stripes with a crayon or marker. Draw a smile with black crayon or marker.

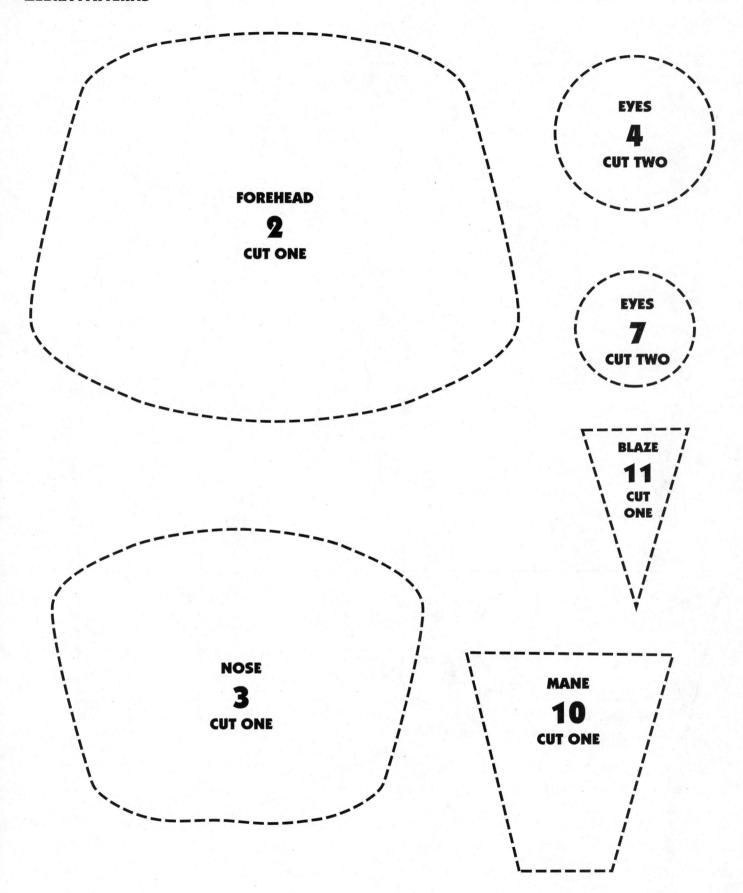

FOREHEAD
2
CUT ONE

EYES
4
CUT TWO

EYES
7
CUT TWO

BLAZE
11
CUT
ONE

NOSE
3
CUT ONE

MANE
10
CUT ONE

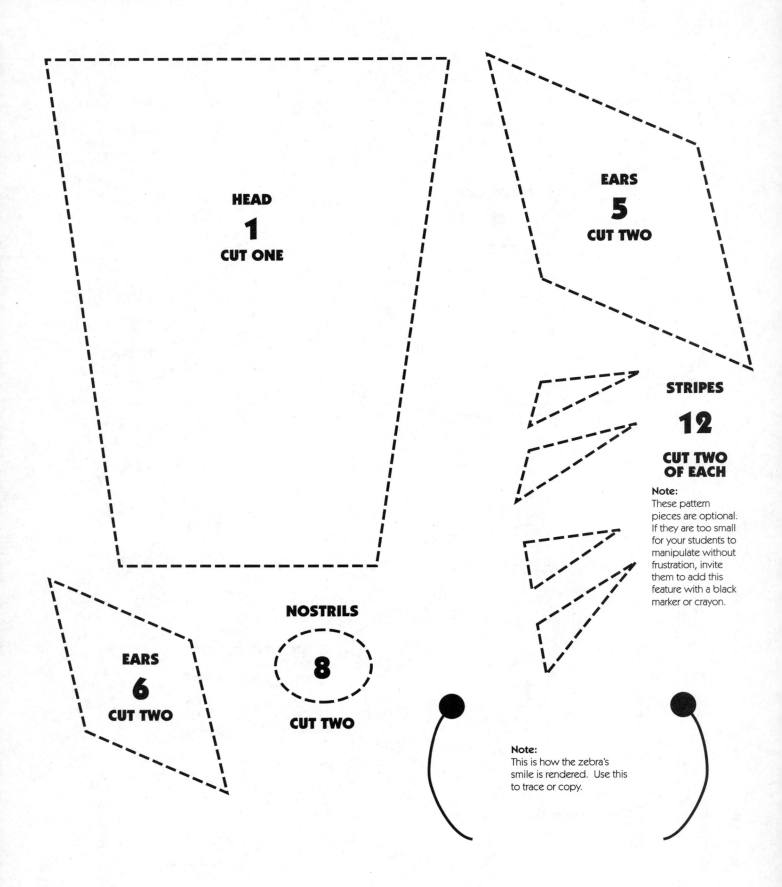

HEAD

1

CUT ONE

EARS

5

CUT TWO

STRIPES

12

CUT TWO OF EACH

Note:
These pattern pieces are optional. If they are too small for your students to manipulate without frustration, invite them to add this feature with a black marker or crayon.

EARS

6

CUT TWO

NOSTRILS

8

CUT TWO

Note:
This is how the zebra's smile is rendered. Use this to trace or copy.

Materials: *black, white and yellow paper; scissors; glue; black crayon or marker*

PENGUIN

1 Cut one #1 body from white paper.

2 Cut two #2 sides from black paper and glue them to either side of the body.

3 Cut two #3 feet from black paper and glue them to the underside of the body.

4 Cut two #4 wings from black paper and glue them to the underside of the body as shown. Cut one #5 eye from white paper and glue it to the top, center of the body.

5 Cut one #6 bill from yellow paper and glue it to the body in front of the #5 eye.

6 Cut one #7 eye from black paper and glue it to the center of the #5 eye. Use a black crayon or marker and draw a smile on the penguin.

PENGUIN PATTERNS

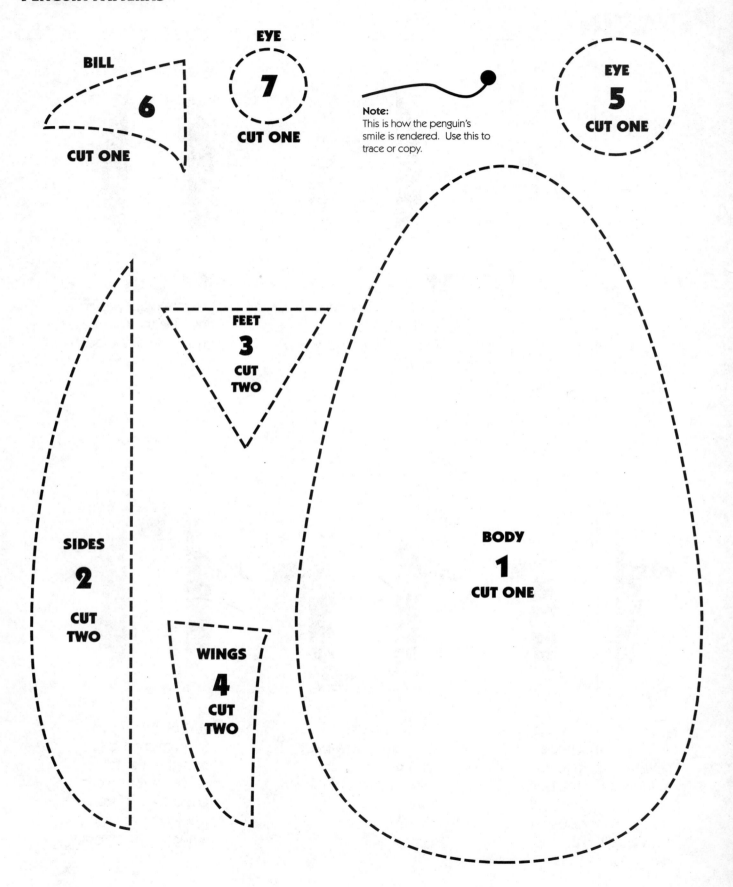

BILL

6

CUT ONE

EYE

7

CUT ONE

Note:
This is how the penguin's smile is rendered. Use this to trace or copy.

EYE

5

CUT ONE

FEET

3

CUT TWO

SIDES

2

CUT TWO

WINGS

4

CUT TWO

BODY

1

CUT ONE

WOLF

Materials: *tan, brown, yellow, black and pink paper; scissors; glue; black crayon or marker*

1 Cut one #1 head from tan paper. Cut one #2 nose from brown paper and glue it to the head as shown.

2 Cut one #3 mouth from pink paper and glue it to the head as shown.

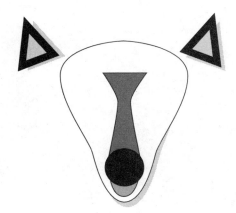

3 Cut two #4 ears from black paper. Cut two #5 ears from brown paper. Glue the #5 ears, centered, to the #4 ears. Cut one #6 nose from black paper and glue it to the bottom of the #2 nose.

4 Cut one #7 forehead from brown paper and glue it to the top of the head. Glue the ears, as shown, to the top of the forehead.

5 Cut two #8 eyes from white paper and glue them to the wolf's head as shown.

6 Cut two #9 manes from brown paper and glue them to the underside of the head. Cut two #10 eyes from yellow paper and glue them to the center of the #8 eyes. Add a pupil with black crayon or marker.

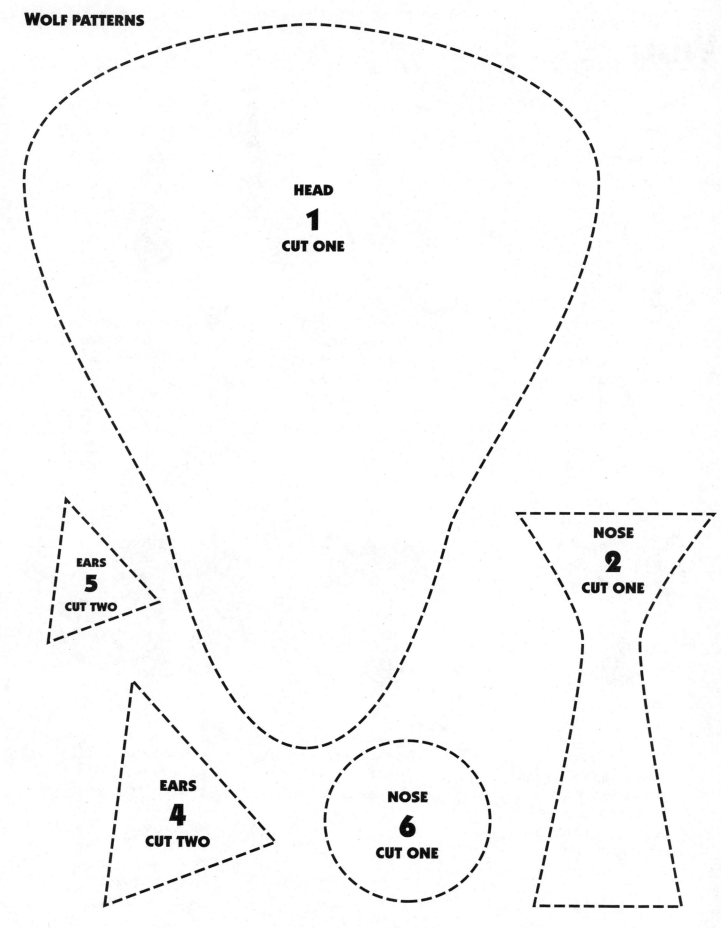

HEAD
1
CUT ONE

NOSE
2
CUT ONE

EARS
5
CUT TWO

EARS
4
CUT TWO

NOSE
6
CUT ONE

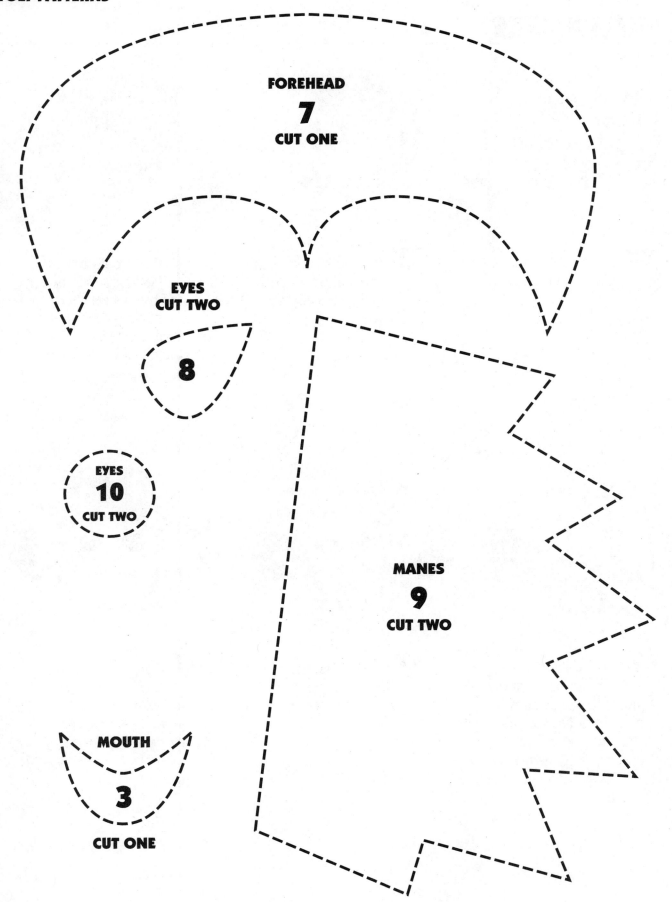

FOREHEAD
7
CUT ONE

EYES
CUT TWO

8

EYES
10
CUT TWO

MANES
9
CUT TWO

MOUTH
3
CUT ONE

Materials: *brown, tan and black paper; scissors; glue*

CHIMPANZEE

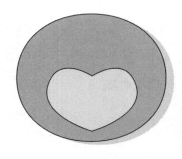

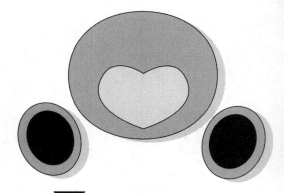

▼**1** Cut one #1 head from brown paper.

▼**2** Cut one #2 mask from tan paper and glue it to the head as shown.

▼**3** Cut two #3 ears from brown paper. Cut two #4 ears from black paper and glue them to the center of the #3 ears.

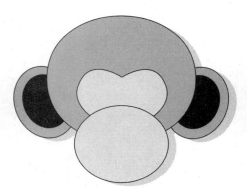

▼**4** Cut one #5 mouth from tan paper and glue it to the bottom of the head as shown. Glue the ears to the underside of the head as shown.

▼**5** Cut two #6 eyes from black paper and glue them to the mask.

▼**6** Cut two #7 nostrils and glue them to the #5 mouth as shown. Add a smile to the chimpanzee with black crayon or marker.

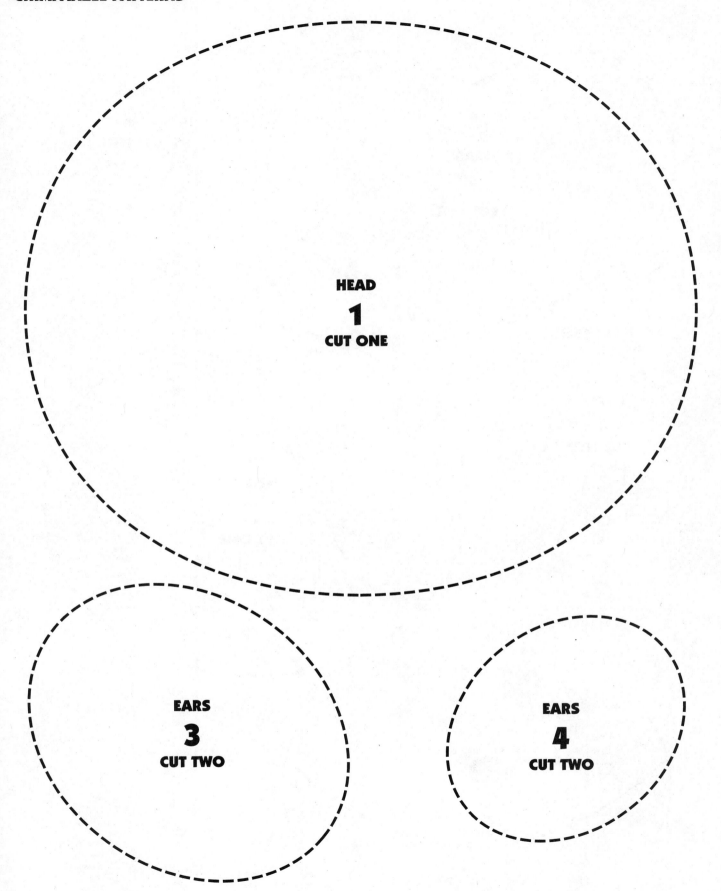

HEAD
1
CUT ONE

EARS
3
CUT TWO

EARS
4
CUT TWO

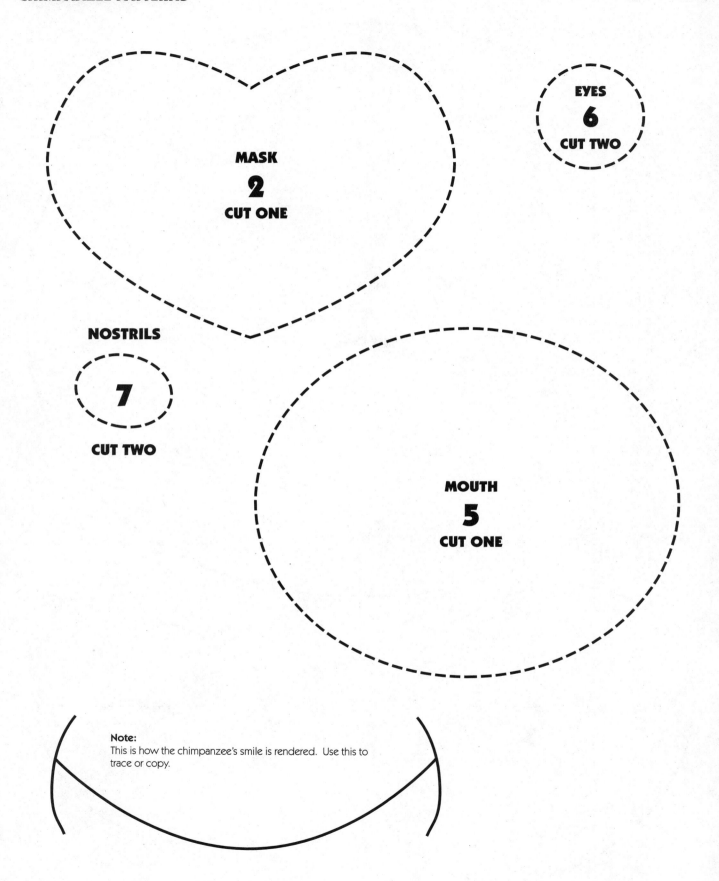

MASK

2

CUT ONE

EYES

6

CUT TWO

NOSTRILS

7

CUT TWO

MOUTH

5

CUT ONE

Note:
This is how the chimpanzee's smile is rendered. Use this to trace or copy.

Materials: white, gray and black paper; scissors; glue; black crayon or marker

MOUNTAIN GOAT

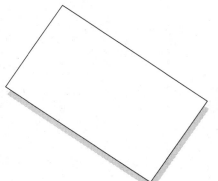

1 Cut one #1 head from white paper.

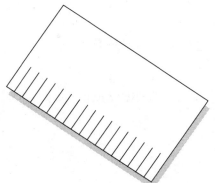

2 Make several cuts in the head with scissors as shown. This will create the "goatee."

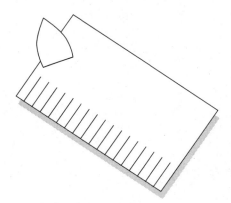

3 Cut one #2 ear from white paper and glue it to the head as shown.

4 Cut one #3 ear from black paper and glue it to the bottom center of the #2 ear.

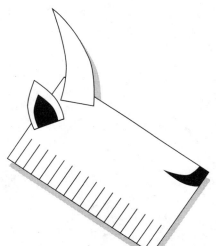

5 Cut one #4 horn from gray paper and glue it to the top of the head as shown. Cut one #5 nose from black paper and glue it to the top right corner of the head as shown.

6 Cut one #6 eye from black paper and glue it to the head. If this piece is too small for your students to manipulate, add this detail with black crayon or marker. Add a smile with black crayon or marker.

MOUNTAIN GOAT PATTERNS

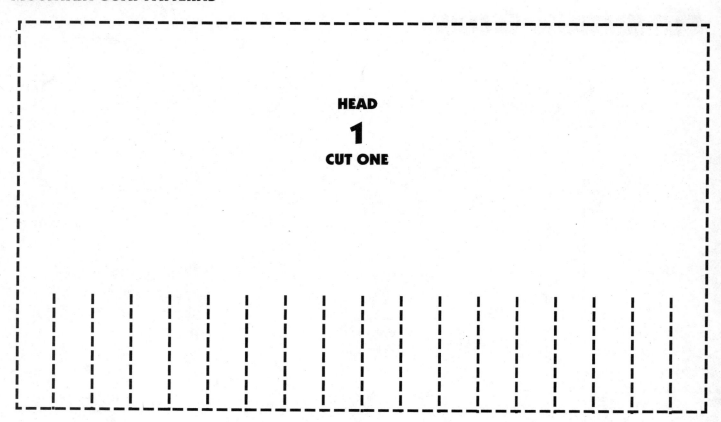

HEAD

1

CUT ONE

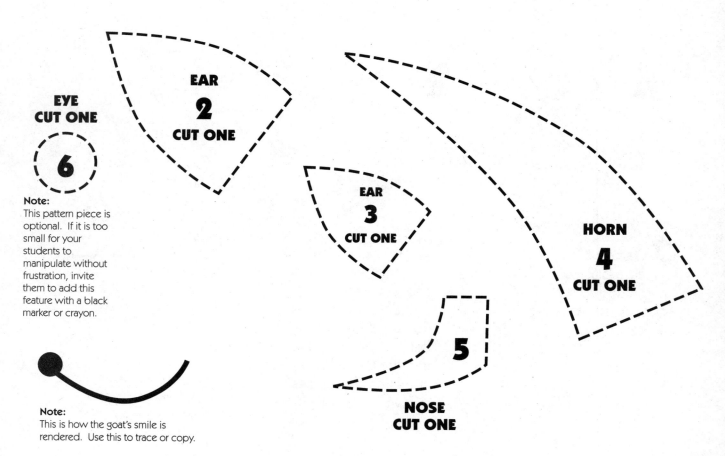

EYE
CUT ONE

6

Note:
This pattern piece is
optional. If it is too
small for your
students to
manipulate without
frustration, invite
them to add this
feature with a black
marker or crayon.

EAR

2

CUT ONE

EAR

3

CUT ONE

HORN

4

CUT ONE

5

NOSE
CUT ONE

Note:
This is how the goat's smile is
rendered. Use this to trace or copy.

Materials: *yellow, brown and black paper; scissors; glue; black and brown crayons or markers*

GIRAFFE

1 Cut one #1 head from yellow paper. Cut one #2 neck from yellow paper. Glue the head to the neck as shown.

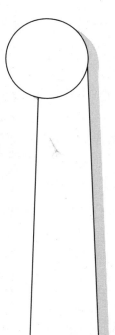

2 Cut one #3 nose from yellow paper and glue it to the underside of #1 head as shown. Cut one #4 ear from brown paper. Cut one #5 ear from black paper and glue it, centered, to the #4 ear. This detail can also be added with black crayon or marker.

3 Cut one #6 muzzle from yellow paper and glue it to the #3 nose as shown. Cut one #7 mane from brown paper and fringe it along the length of one side. Glue it to the underside of the neck. Glue the ear to the top of the head.

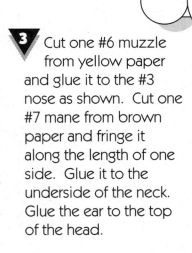

4 Cut one #8 antler from brown paper and glue it to the top of the head. The #9 spots can either be cut from brown paper and glued to the giraffe as shown *or* your students can add the spots with a brown marker or crayon. Cut one #11 eye and one #10 nostril from black paper and glue them to the giraffe as shown. Again, these pieces may be added with marker or crayon. Add a smile with black crayon or marker.

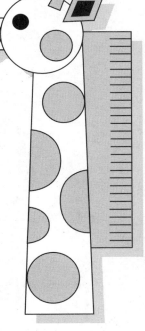

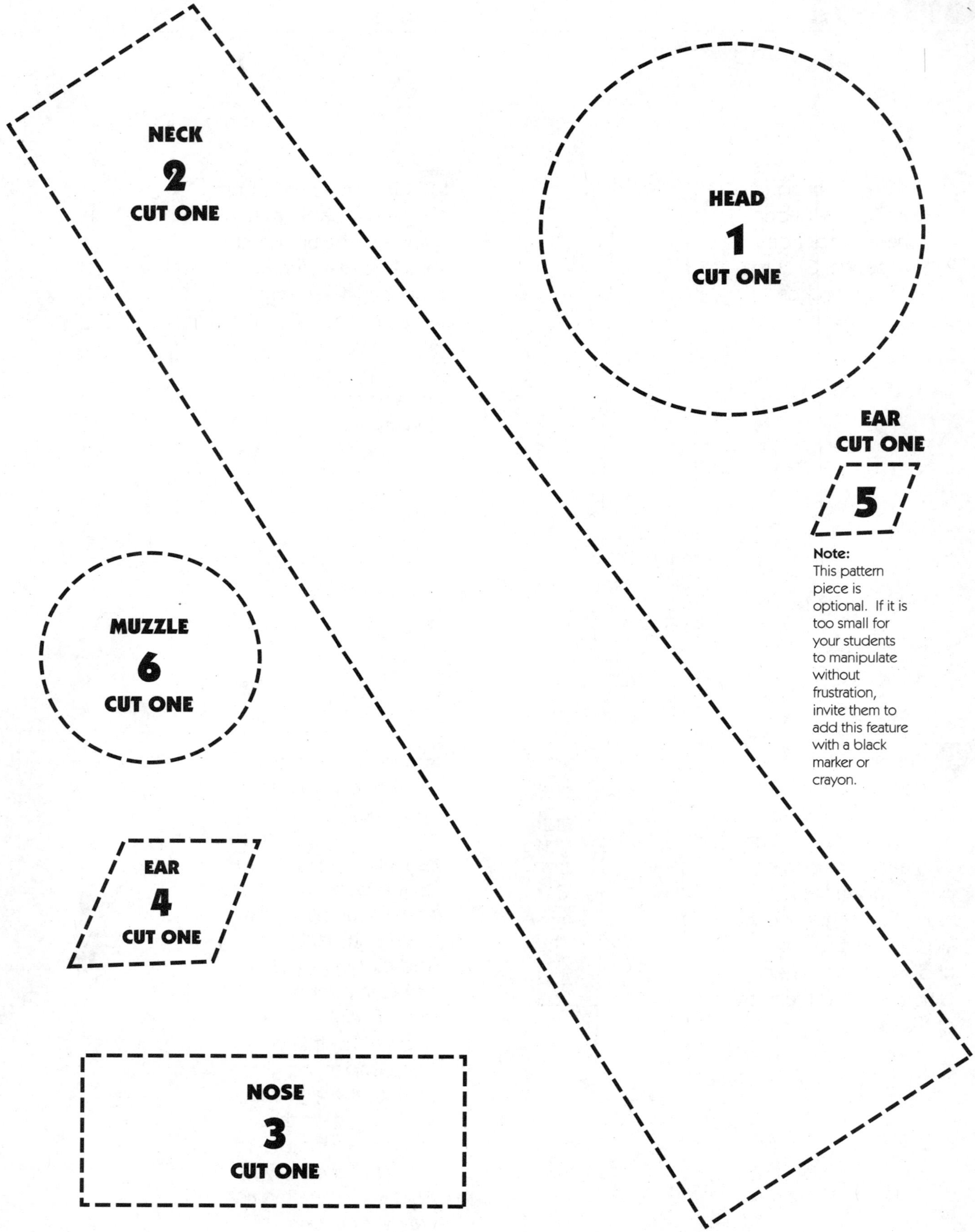

GIRAFFE PATTERNS

NECK

2

CUT ONE

HEAD

1

CUT ONE

EAR
CUT ONE

5

Note:
This pattern
piece is
optional. If it is
too small for
your students
to manipulate
without
frustration,
invite them to
add this feature
with a black
marker or
crayon.

MUZZLE

6

CUT ONE

EAR

4

CUT ONE

NOSE

3

CUT ONE

GIRAFFE PATTERNS

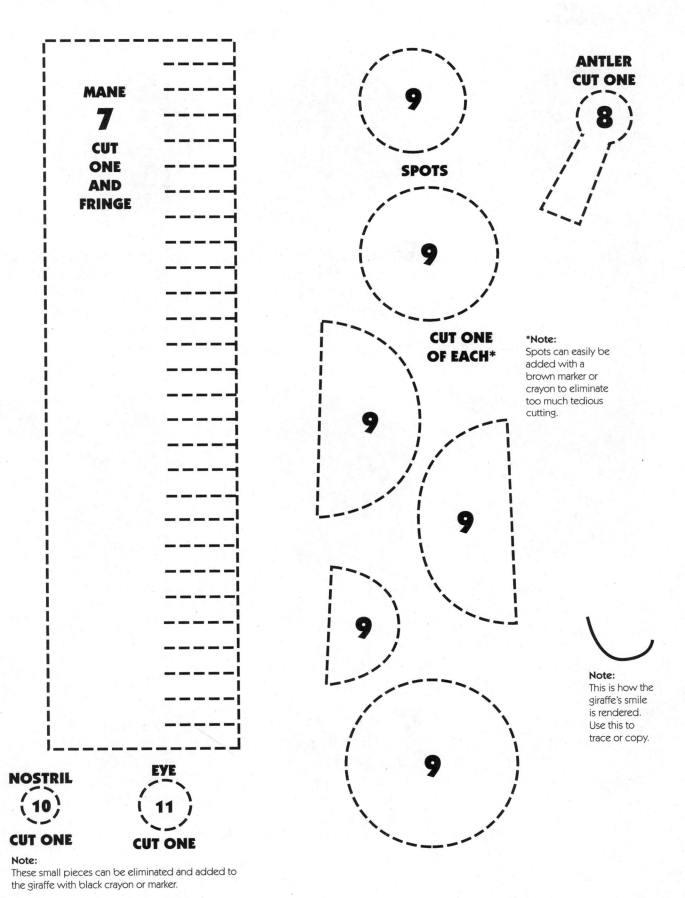

MANE
7
CUT
ONE
AND
FRINGE

SPOTS

9

9

ANTLER
CUT ONE
8

CUT ONE
OF EACH*

9

9

9

9

*Note:
Spots can easily be added with a brown marker or crayon to eliminate too much tedious cutting.

Note:
This is how the giraffe's smile is rendered. Use this to trace or copy.

NOSTRIL
10
CUT ONE

EYE
11
CUT ONE

Note:
These small pieces can be eliminated and added to the giraffe with black crayon or marker.

TLC10010 Copyright © Teaching & Learning Company, Carthage, IL 62321

Materials: *brown, black and white paper; scissors; glue; black crayon or marker*
Optional Materials: *pipe cleaners or broom straw*

WALRUS

1 Cut one #1 head from brown paper.

2 Cut one #2 nose from brown paper and glue it to the head as shown. Cut two #3 eyes from black paper and glue them to the head as shown.

3 Cut one #4 muzzle from brown paper and glue it to the bottom of the head, overlapping the #2 nose as shown.

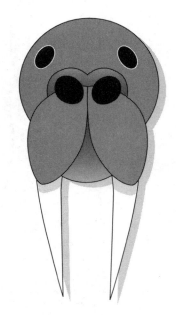

4 Cut two #5 lips from brown paper and glue them to the muzzle.

5 Cut two #6 nostrils from black paper and glue them to the head as shown. Cut two #7 tusks from white paper and glue them to the underside of the lips.

6 Draw some "freckles" on the walrus's face and glue on some broom straw or pipe cleaners for whiskers.

WALRUS PATTERNS

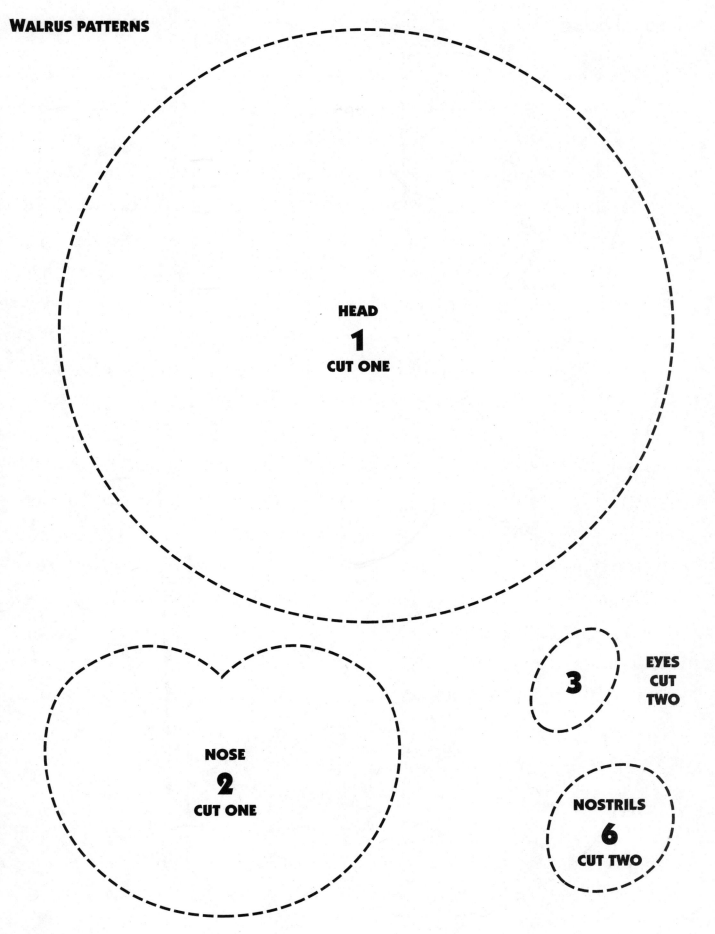

HEAD

1

CUT ONE

NOSE

2

CUT ONE

EYES
CUT
TWO

3

NOSTRILS

6

CUT TWO

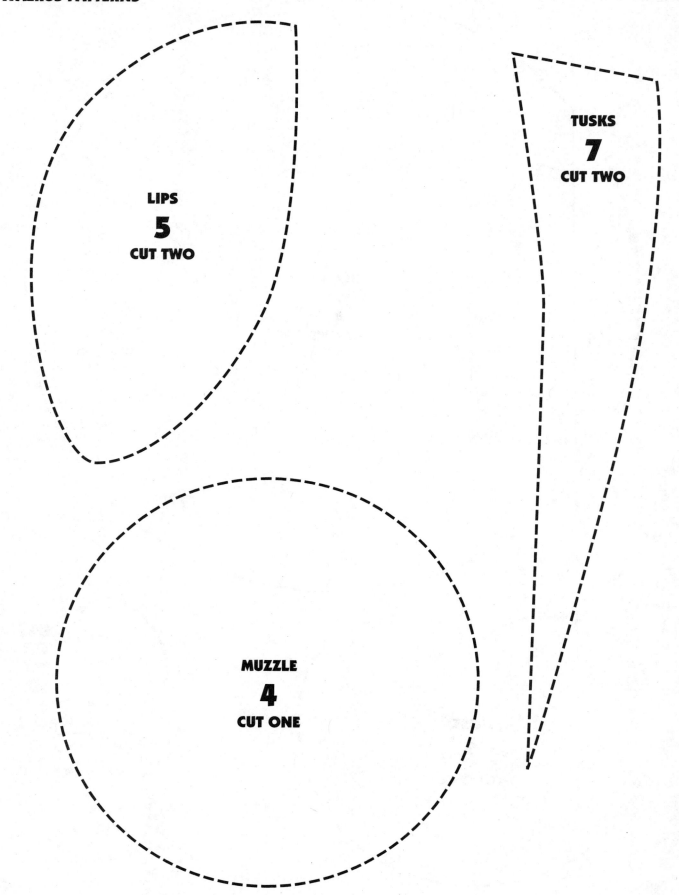

LIPS
5
CUT TWO

TUSKS
7
CUT TWO

MUZZLE
4
CUT ONE

Materials: *tan and black paper, scissors, glue, black crayon or marker, yarn scraps*

CAMEL

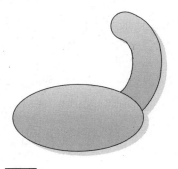

1 Cut one #1 body from tan paper.

2 Cut one #2 neck from tan paper and glue it to the underside of the body.

3 Cut one #3 head from tan paper and glue it to the underside of the neck. Cut two #4 humps from tan paper and glue them to the underside of the body.

4 Cut one #5 ear from tan paper. Cut one #6 ear from black paper and glue it, centered, to the #5 ear. This detail can also be added with marker (see note on pattern page). Cut four #7 legs from tan paper and begin gluing them to the underside of the camel's body.

5 Finish gluing the four legs to the camel. Glue the ear to the camel's head as shown. Cut one #8 nostril and one #9 eye from black paper. Glue them to the head as shown. These details can also be added with black crayon or marker.

6 Glue a yarn scrap to the tail end of the camel for a tail. Add a smile with black crayon or marker.

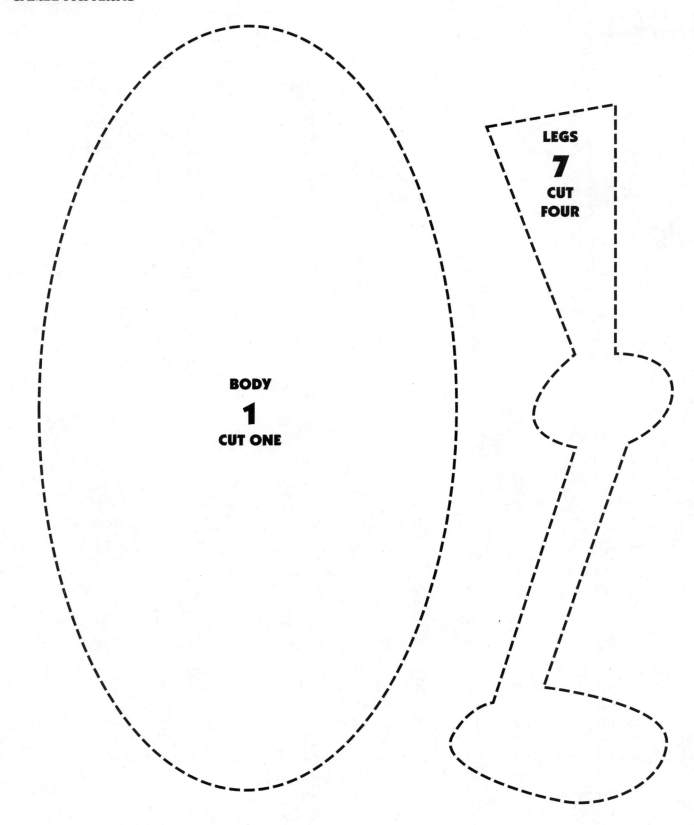

LEGS

7

CUT FOUR

BODY

1

CUT ONE

CAMEL PATTERNS

Note:
These pattern pieces are optional. If they are too small for your students to manipulate without frustration, invite them to add these features with a black marker or crayon.

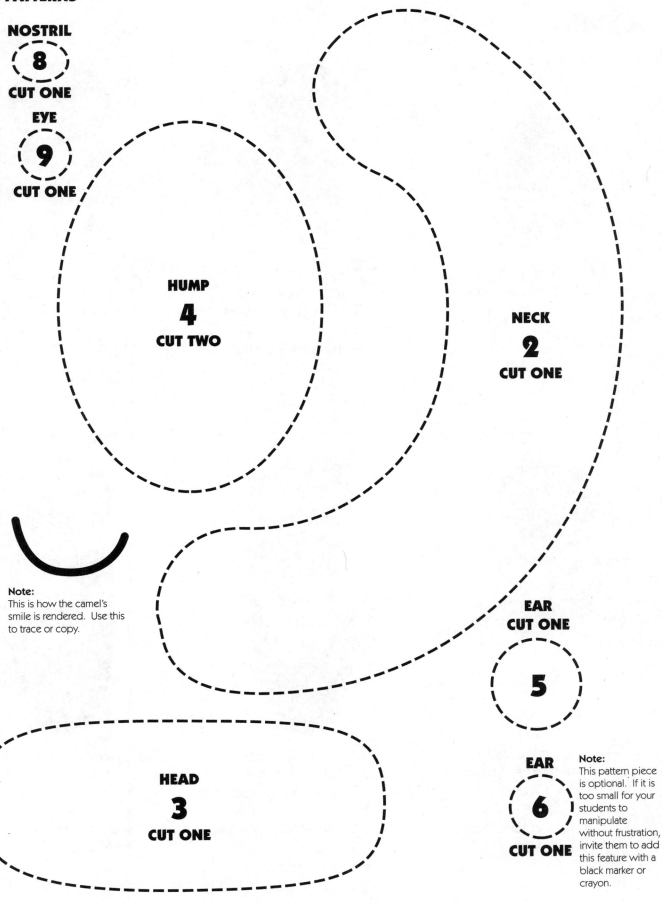

NOSTRIL

8

CUT ONE

EYE

9

CUT ONE

HUMP

4

CUT TWO

NECK

2

CUT ONE

Note:
This is how the camel's smile is rendered. Use this to trace or copy.

EAR
CUT ONE

5

HEAD

3

CUT ONE

EAR

6

CUT ONE

Note:
This pattern piece is optional. If it is too small for your students to manipulate without frustration, invite them to add this feature with a black marker or crayon.

OWL

Materials: black, brown and yellow paper; scissors; glue; black crayon or marker

1 Cut one #1 body from brown paper.

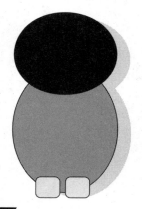

2 Cut one #2 head from black paper. Glue it to the body as shown. Cut two #3 talons from yellow paper and glue them to the bottom of the body.

3 Cut one #4 head from brown paper and glue it, centered, to the #2 head. Cut two #5 eyes from yellow paper. Cut two #6 eyes from black paper and glue them, centered, to the #5 eyes.

4 Glue the eyes to the head as shown. Cut one #7 beak from black paper and glue it to the center of the head between the eyes.

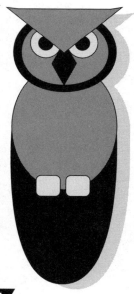

5 Cut one #8 crest from brown paper and glue it to the top half of the head. Cut one #9 tail from black paper and glue it to the underside of the body.

6 With black crayon or marker, add two vertical lines to each talon to create "claws." Create "feathers" on the breast of the owl by drawing lines as shown.

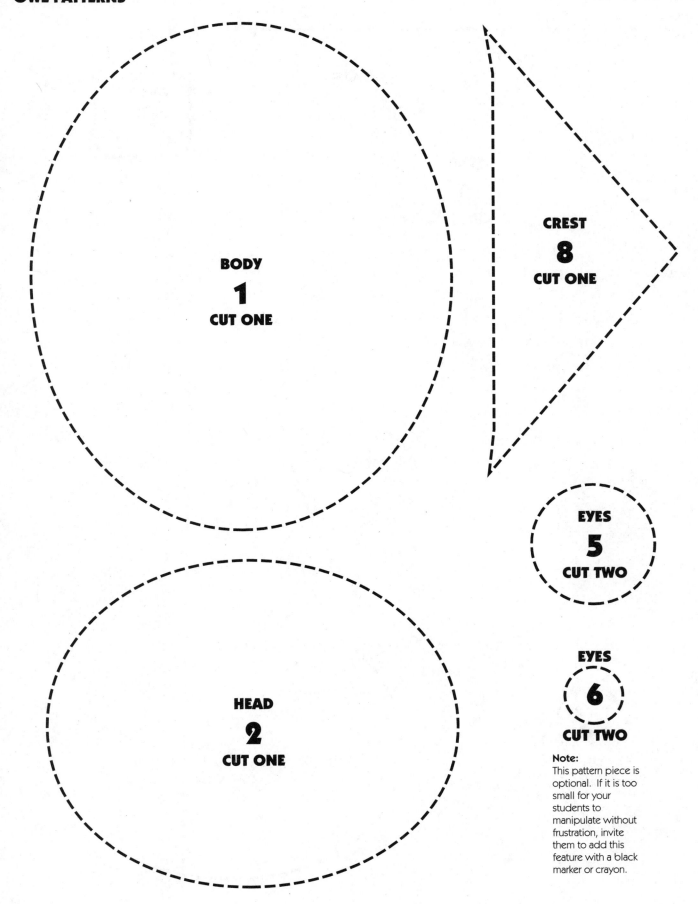

BODY

1

CUT ONE

CREST

8

CUT ONE

HEAD

2

CUT ONE

EYES

5

CUT TWO

EYES

6

CUT TWO

Note:
This pattern piece is optional. If it is too small for your students to manipulate without frustration, invite them to add this feature with a black marker or crayon.

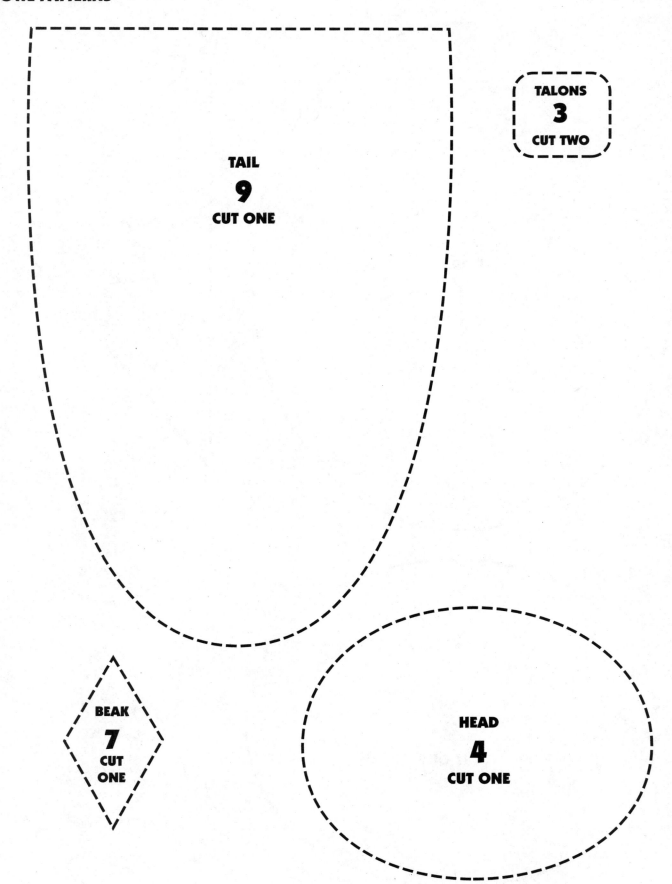

TALONS
3
CUT TWO

TAIL
9
CUT ONE

BEAK
7
CUT
ONE

HEAD
4
CUT ONE

OCTOPUS

Materials: *light blue, white and black paper; scissors; glue; black marker or crayon*

1 Cut one #1 body from light blue paper.

2 Cut one #2 head from light blue paper and glue it to the body as shown.

3 Cut two #3 eyes from white paper and glue them to the head as shown. Cut two #4 legs from light blue paper and glue them to the body.

4 Cut two #5 legs from light blue paper and glue them to the body beneath the #4 legs. Cut two #6 eyes from black paper and glue them to the bottom center of the #3 eyes.

5 Cut two #7 legs from light blue paper and glue them to the body next to the #5 legs. Cut two #8 legs from light blue paper and glue them next to the #7 legs.

6 Add a smile with a black marker or crayon.

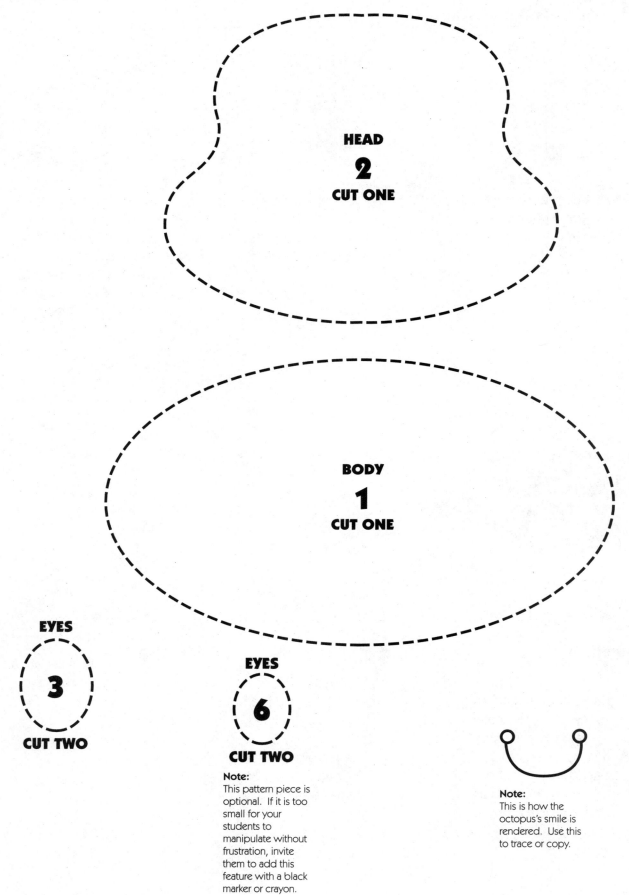

HEAD

2

CUT ONE

BODY

1

CUT ONE

EYES

3

CUT TWO

EYES

6

CUT TWO

Note:
This pattern piece is optional. If it is too small for your students to manipulate without frustration, invite them to add this feature with a black marker or crayon.

Note:
This is how the octopus's smile is rendered. Use this to trace or copy.

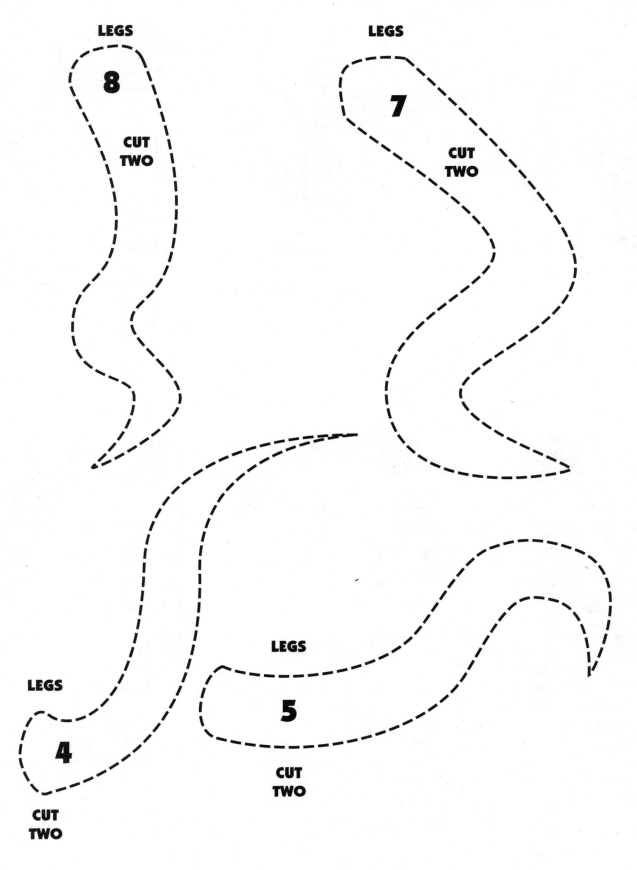

LEGS

8

CUT
TWO

LEGS

7

CUT
TWO

LEGS

LEGS

4

5

CUT
TWO

CUT
TWO

Materials: *green, red and black paper; scissors; glue; black crayon or marker*

RED-EYED TREE TOAD

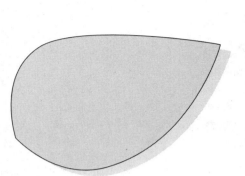

1 Cut one #1 leaf from green paper.

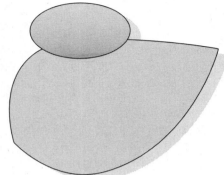

2 Cut one #2 head from green paper and glue it to the leaf as shown.

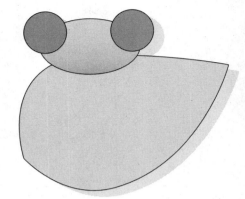

3 Cut two #3 eyes from red paper. Glue them to the head as shown.

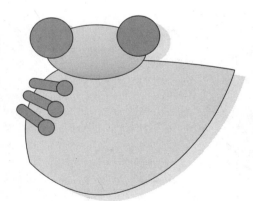

4 Cut six #4 fingers from red paper. Glue the first set of three to the leaf as shown.

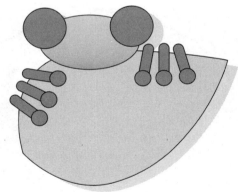

5 Glue the second set of three fingers to the leaf as shown.

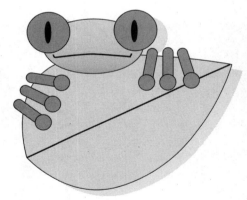

6 Cut two #5 pupils from black paper and glue them, centered, to the eyes. Draw a smile on the toad with a black crayon or marker.

LEAF

1

CUT ONE

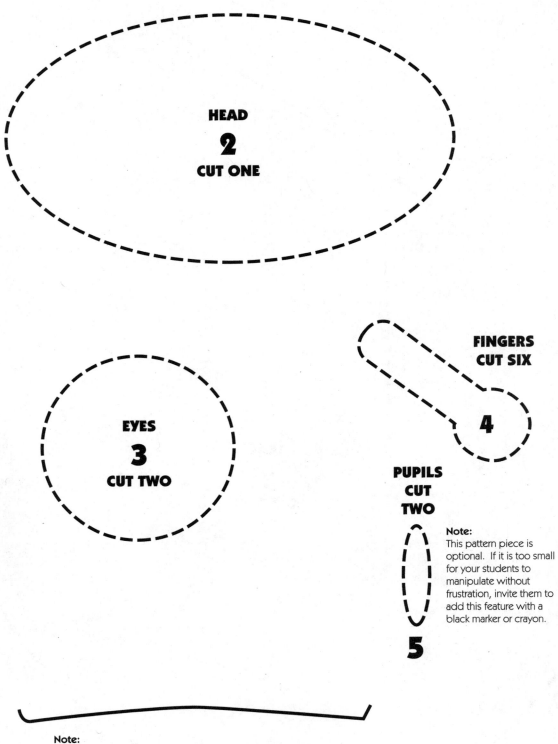

HEAD
2
CUT ONE

EYES
3
CUT TWO

FINGERS
CUT SIX
4

PUPILS
CUT
TWO

Note:
This pattern piece is optional. If it is too small for your students to manipulate without frustration, invite them to add this feature with a black marker or crayon.

5

Note:
This is how the frog's mouth is rendered. Use this to trace or copy.

COBRA

Materials: *green, yellow, black and red paper; scissors; glue; black crayon or markers*

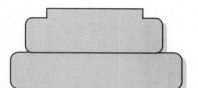

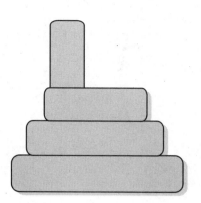

1 Cut one #1 body from green paper. Cut one #2 body from green paper and glue it to the #1 body.

2 Cut one #3 body from green paper and glue it to the #2 body. Cut one #4 neck from green paper and glue it to the #3 body as shown.

3 Cut one #5 head from green paper and glue it to the #4 neck. Cut two #6 eyes from yellow paper and glue them to the head as shown.

4 Cut one #7 hood from black paper. Cut one #8 hood from yellow paper and glue it, centered, to the #7 hood. Cut one #9 mouth from red paper and glue it to the cobra's head as shown.

5 Glue the hood to the back of the cobra's head. Add nostrils, fangs and circles to the eyes with a black crayon or marker. Add horizontal stripes to the hood using a black crayon or marker.

6 Add the triangular-shaped pattern to the cobra using either pattern piece #10 or a black crayon or marker.

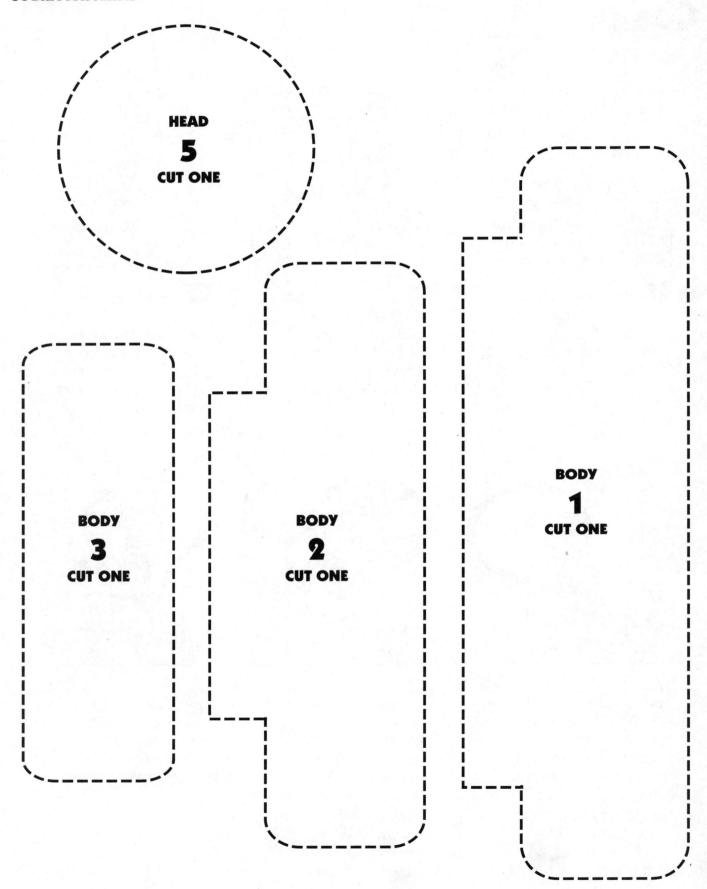

HEAD
5
CUT ONE

BODY
3
CUT ONE

BODY
2
CUT ONE

BODY
1
CUT ONE

COBRA PATTERNS

EYES
6
CUT TWO

HOOD
7
CUT ONE

Note:
The cobra shows 18 triangles cut and glued into position. This will become too tedious for most young children. You can either precut these shapes using a paper cutter or invite them to add this detail with black crayon or marker.

MOUTH

9

CUT ONE

HOOD
8
CUT ONE

NECK
4
CUT ONE

SUGGESTIONS FOR USING PATTERNS

OPTION 1

Cut one of each pattern piece. Trace the pieces onto poster board, or any other paper you have that is sturdy, yet thin enough to cut with scissors. Transcribe the information printed on each pattern piece to the poster board pieces. Make as many sets of these as you predict you will need for your groups of students. Invite your students to trace around these pieces onto the appropriate color of paper. You will also need to photocopy the directions page for each Cut and Create zoo animal. Your students can use this for a visual, step-by-step guide to help them "build" their animal. Laminate the directions page to add to their life span. Make as many photocopies of the directions page as you have sets of pattern pieces. Store each set in a Ziploc™ bag.

OPTION 2

Here's a quick and easy suggestion. Use this method when you're in a hurry and preparing a Cut and Create activity for only one or two students. First, tape the pattern page(s) to a window or light box. Hold the appropriate color of paper up to the pattern page and trace the pattern piece, piece number and then indicate how many pieces the student will need to cut of each piece. Both this method and Option 1 allow you to edit out any pieces you feel are too small for your students to successfully manipulate. Photocopy a directions page for each student. Provide them with your tracings, a directions page and the materials listed and they have everything they need to do their project.

OPTION 3

Photocopy the patterns directly onto 8½" x 11" (21.59 x 27.94 cm) colored paper. This will involve some cutting and pasting. Cut apart the pattern page(s) and glue the pattern pieces to be cut from a single color onto one sheet of white paper. Photocopy a set of these pattern pages for each student. You will also need to make several photocopies of the directions page; one for each group of students.

Note: Laminate your students' Cut and Create projects. Use a staple gun to staple them to a paint stick and put them in your drama corner, prop box or next to an appropriate story in your classroom library. Your students will love to role-play and dialogue with these animals!

PATTERNS FOR A CUT AND CREATE ZOO

In order to provide you the maximum number of patterns in two pages, you will need to enlarge these patterns to your desired size.

FOLIAGE

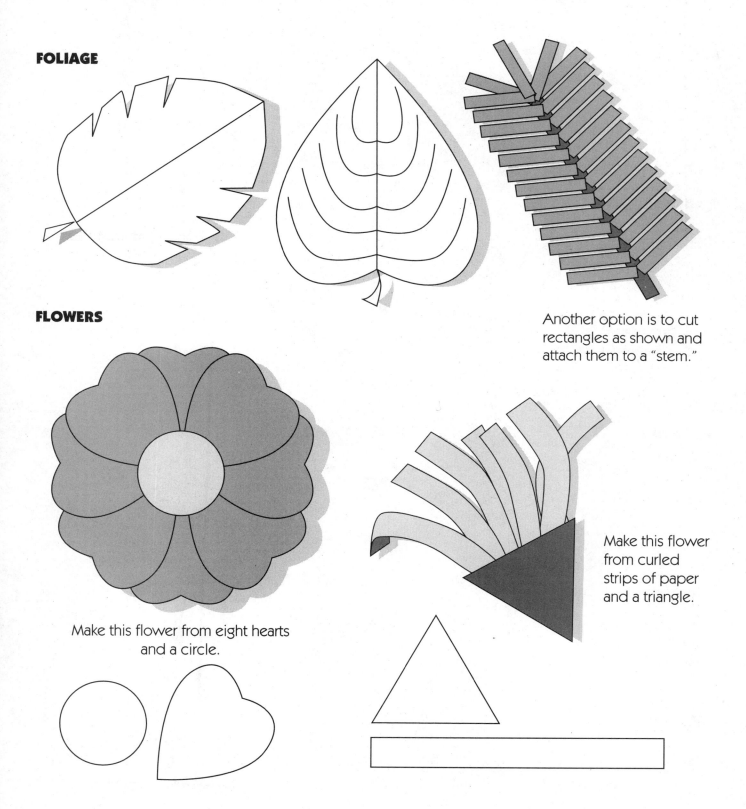

Another option is to cut rectangles as shown and attach them to a "stem."

FLOWERS

Make this flower from eight hearts and a circle.

Make this flower from curled strips of paper and a triangle.

MORE PATTERNS FOR A CUT AND CREATE ZOO

ROCKS

LIMB

UNDER THE SEA

starfish

seaweed

fish

feeding time!

MOUNTAIN

TREE AND SWING

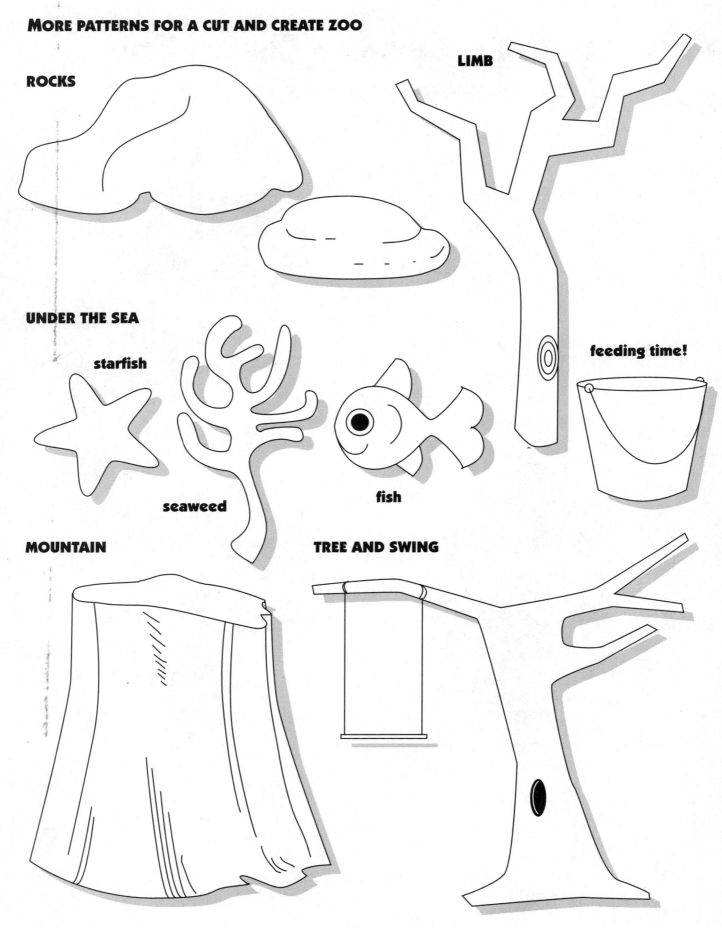